T0089313

THE BREAKFAST BIBLE

KATE M MILLAN

PHOTOGRAPHY BY

SANG AN

weldonowen

CONTENTS

INTRODUCTION

The first meal of the day can be the most important one. It literally "breaks" the "fast" after a night's rest, providing fuel and flavor for both body and mind. Nutrition, favorite ingredients, season, and nostalgia all contribute to our decision of what to eat in the morning, and the choices we make typically go a long way toward setting the tone for the rest of the day. Classics like eggs and bacon, pancakes, waffles, and French toast will never go out of style, and all of them are well represented here, along with plenty of ideas for making them your own. But our morning-table options are also more varied now than ever before.

Many of today's breakfast preferences embrace customs from around the world. In these pages you'll find Mexican-inspired tacos (page 51) and huevos rancheros (page 48), an Asian noodle bowl (page 45), and a flavor-packed North African dish of eggs cooked in a spiced tomato sauce (page 52). Even breakfast sandwiches go beyond the traditional, much-loved bacon-and-egg panini to include morning variations on the banh mi, cubano, and croque madame.

A steadily growing pantry of newly available ingredients and a better understanding of nutrition have also influenced our morning meal. Breakfast bowls come filled with açai berries and other fruits, healthful grains and seeds such as quinoa and chia, fruit-and-nut granola, fiber-rich oatmeal, and noodles. Whole-grain toasts (page 18) are nourishing fare as well, with toppings that range from avocado and winter squash to smoked salmon, each one liberally sprinkled with seasonings. Yogurt parfaits (page 16), another canvas for healthful and delicious creativity, are easily customized with fresh and dried fruits, granola, seeds, and nuts. And the incredible egg, a protein powerhouse, stars in omelets, scrambles, frittatas, and stratas, as well as in breakfast sandwiches and burritos, all of them in a heady mix of guises.

Presenting a wealth of inspired ideas is a central theme of *The Breakfast Bible*. For example, you'll find fresh takes on several traditional breakfast offerings, such as classic buttermilk pancakes with a choice of add-ins and toppings (page 72), crisp puff-pastry tart shells with eight different fruit fillings (page 100), raised doughnuts dressed up with glazes, sugars, and sprinkles (page 97), and basic granola (page 11) tailored to taste with nuts, dried fruits, and other ingredients.

The goal of this diverse collection of recipes and ideas is to provide delicious and thoughtful options for the breakfast cook and for everyone who is lucky enough to be seated at the table. With a complete understanding of the morning classics and of the many variations that can be created from them, what to eat for breakfast becomes the easiest decision of your day.

FRUITS & GRAINS

FRESH FRUIT, YOGURT PARFAITS, SMOOTHIE BOWLS,
GRANOLA, OATMEAL, BREAKFAST TOASTS & MORE

DRIED FRUIT & NUT GRANOLAS

Once you learn the basic method for making homemade granola, endless variations abound. Mix the oats with nuts and spices, pour warm sweetened oil over the top, mix well, and bake in a low oven. Stir in any dried fruits or chocolate after baking. Each of the variations offered here makes about 3½ cups (400 g). Store granola in an airtight container at room temperature for up to 2 weeks or in the freezer for up to 1 month.

almond granola with apricots

Preheat the oven to 300°F (150°C). Coat a baking sheet with nonstick cooking spray.

In a large bowl, stir together the oats, almonds, flaxseeds, cinnamon, and salt. Set aside. In a saucepan, combine the brown sugar, honey, coconut oil, and vanilla. Place over medium heat and cook, stirring occasionally, until smooth, 2–3 minutes. Pour over the oat mixture and stir to combine. Spread the mixture out on the prepared baking sheet.

Bake, stirring twice and rotating the pan once, until the granola is golden, about 25 minutes. Let cool completely on the baking sheet, then stir in the dried apricots.

Nonstick cooking spray
2 cups (185 g) rolled oats
¾ cup (115 g) chopped raw almonds
2 tbsp flaxseeds
1 tsp ground cinnamon
¼ tsp salt
½ cup (105 g) firmly packed light brown sugar
⅓ cup (125 g) honey
¼ cup (60 ml) coconut oil
2 tsp pure vanilla extract
¾ cup (140 g) dried apricots, chopped

peanutty granola with blueberries

Preheat the oven to 300°F (150°C). Coat a baking sheet with nonstick cooking spray.

In a bowl, stir together the oats, almonds, and salt; set aside. In a saucepan, combine the coconut oil, peanut butter, and maple syrup. Warm over medium heat, stirring often, until smooth, 2–3 minutes. Pour over the oat mixture and stir to combine. Spread the mixture out on the prepared baking sheet.

Bake, stirring twice and rotating the pan once, until the granola is golden, about 25 minutes. Let cool completely on the baking sheet, then stir in the dried blueberries.

Nonstick cooking spray
2 cups (185 g) rolled oats
½ cup (85 g) chopped raw almonds
½ tsp salt
¼ cup (60 ml) coconut oil
¼ cup (75 g) smooth peanut butter
¼ cup (85 g) pure maple syrup
⅓ cup (40 g) dried blueberries

maple-pecan granola with toasted coconut & cranberries

Preheat the oven to 300°F (150°C). Coat a baking sheet with nonstick cooking spray.

In a large bowl, stir together the oats, pecans, cinnamon, and salt. Set aside. In a saucepan, combine the maple syrup, coconut oil, and vanilla. Place over medium heat and cook, stirring occasionally, until smooth. Pour over the oat mixture and stir to combine. Spread the mixture out on the prepared baking sheet.

Bake, stirring twice and rotating the pan once, until the granola is golden, about 25 minutes. Let cool completely on the baking sheet, then stir in the dried cranberries and coconut flakes.

Nonstick cooking spray
2 cups (185 g) rolled oats
½ cup (60 g) pecans, chopped
1 tsp ground cinnamon
¼ tsp salt
½ cup (170 g) pure maple syrup
¼ cup (60 ml) coconut oil
1½ tsp pure vanilla extract
½ cup (60 g) dried cranberries
⅓ cup (30 g) unsweetened flaked coconut

honey granola with cherries, walnuts & chocolate

Preheat the oven to 300°F (150°C). Coat a baking sheet with nonstick cooking spray.

In a large bowl, stir together the oats, walnuts, cinnamon, and salt. Set aside. In a saucepan, combine the brown sugar, honey, coconut oil, and vanilla. Place over medium heat and cook, stirring occasionally, until smooth. Pour over the oat mixture and stir to combine. Spread the mixture out on the prepared baking sheet.

Bake, stirring twice and rotating the pan once, until the granola is golden, about 25 minutes. Let cool completely on the baking sheet, then stir in the dried cherries and chocolate chips.

Nonstick cooking spray
2 cups (185 g) rolled oats
½ cup (60 g) walnuts, chopped
1 tsp ground cinnamon
½ tsp salt
½ cup (105 g) firmly packed light brown sugar
⅓ cup (60 g) honey
¼ cup (60 ml) coconut oil
1 tsp pure vanilla extract
½ cup (60 g) dried cherries
⅓ cup (60 g) semisweet chocolate chips

OLD-FASHIONED OATMEAL

SERVES 4

There's a good reason oatmeal is such a welcome and satisfying breakfast option: it's healthy, hearty, and comes together quickly. Since you can dress it up so many different ways, oatmeal can be enjoyed several days a week. Serving oatmeal with warm milk makes it irresistibly creamy.

¼ tsp salt

2 cups (185 g) rolled oats

1 cup (240 ml) whole milk, half-and-half, or heavy cream, warmed

In a saucepan, combine 3¼ cups (810 ml) water and the salt. Place over high heat and bring to a boil, then stir in the oats. Reduce the heat to medium and cook, stirring occasionally, until the oatmeal is creamy, about 5 minutes. Divide among 4 bowls, top each with ¼ cup (60 ml) milk, and serve.

VARIATIONS

Brown Sugar, Bananas & Fresh Figs
Top each bowl of oatmeal with 1 tbsp dark brown sugar, ½ sliced banana, 2 stemmed and quartered fresh figs, and 1 tbsp pure maple syrup.

Strawberry-Rhubarb Slump
Before preparing the oatmeal, in a heavy saucepan, combine 2 large stalks rhubarb, cut into ½-inch (12-mm) pieces, 1 cup (125 g) strawberries, ⅓ cup (90 g) sugar, and ¼ cup

(60 ml) water. Place over medium heat and cook, stirring occasionally, until the rhubarb is soft, about 10 minutes. Let cool slightly. When the oatmeal is ready, stir in the milk and top each bowl with a generous spoonful of the slump.

Coconut, Dates, Cashews & Honey
Top each bowl of oatmeal with 1 tbsp unsweetened flaked coconut, 2 pitted and sliced dates, 1 tbsp toasted unsalted cashews, and 1 tbsp honey.

CHIA PUDDING WITH KIWI, BLACKBERRIES, APRICOTS & POMEGRANATE

SERVES 4

Loaded with fiber, protein, and omega-3 fatty acids, chia seeds are among the most nutritious foods you can eat and make a great choice for breakfast. Let them plump in liquid (such as the almond milk here) overnight, then spoon them into bowls and top with fresh fruit in the morning.

1 cup (240 ml) almond milk, coconut milk, or a combination

¼ cup (40 g) chia seeds

2 tbsp pure maple syrup

1 tsp pure vanilla extract

1 cup (150 g) blackberries

2 kiwifruits, peeled and sliced

4 ripe apricots, pitted and cut into wedges

½ cup (75 g) pomegranate seeds or raspberries

¼ cup (20 g) toasted coconut chips

In a covered container, stir together the almond milk, chia seeds, maple syrup, and vanilla. Cover and refrigerate for at least 4 hours or up to overnight.

Stir the chia mixture and let stand at room temperature until the seeds are plumped, about 10 minutes. Divide the mixture among 4 serving bowls and arrange the blackberries, kiwi, apricots, and pomegranate seeds on top. Sprinkle evenly with the coconut chips and serve.

Chia seeds plump well in any type of
liquid. Try bright-flavored fruit juices,
such as orange, berry, or pomegranate,
or uncommon nut milks such as those
made from macadamias or cashews.

FRUITY YOGURT PARFAITS

A perfect breakfast on the go, parfaits can be made in advance and refrigerated. Layer the yogurt and granola or fruit in mason jars for an easily totable solution, or arrange the mix in clear glasses or bowls for a sit-down breakfast. Each one of these simple recipes makes enough to serve four.

blood orange, lemon curd, goji berries & pistachios

Divide one-half of the lemon curd among 4 glasses, then layer on half of the oranges, yogurt, and goji berries. Top with the remaining curd, oranges, yogurt, and goji berries. Sprinkle with the pistachios and serve.

1 cup (250 g) lemon curd

3 blood oranges, peeled and cut into slices

3 cups (750 g) plain Greek yogurt

¼ cup (30 g) goji berries or golden raisins

¼ cup (30 g) chopped pistachios

pineapple, papaya, currants & wheat germ

In a bowl, stir together the pineapple, papaya, currants, and lime juice. Divide half of the yogurt among 4 glasses, then layer on half of the fruit mixture. Top with the remaining yogurt and then the remaining fruit. Sprinkle with the wheat germ and serve.

1½ cups (280 g) pineapple cubes

1½ cups (280 g) papaya cubes

3 tbsp currants

2 tbsp fresh lime juice

3 cups (750 g) plain Greek yogurt

3 tbsp toasted wheat germ

honey-raspberry sauce, blueberries & granola

In a small bowl, combine the raspberries, honey, and vanilla. Mash with the back of a fork until chunky and well mixed. Divide the berry mixture equally among four glasses, spoon the yogurt on top, then layer each one equally with the granola and blueberries.

1 cup (120 g) fresh raspberries or chopped fresh strawberries

2 tbsp honey

1 tsp vanilla extract

2 cups (500 g) plain Greek yogurt

1 cup (150 g) granola

1 cup (150 g) blueberries or blackberries

cinnamon apples & pears with walnuts & crystallized ginger

In a large frying pan, melt the butter over medium-high heat, then cook until it begins to brown, about 2 minutes. Add the apples, pears, and cinnamon and cook, stirring occasionally, until the fruit softens but still holds its shape, about 4 minutes. Let cool for a few minutes. Divide half of the yogurt among 4 glasses, then layer on half of the fruit mixture. Top with the remaining yogurt and then the remaining fruit. Sprinkle with the walnuts and crystallized ginger and serve.

2 tbsp unsalted butter

2 Granny Smith apples, peeled, cored, and cut into ¼-inch (6-mm) pieces

2 pears, peeled, cored, and cut into ¼-inch (6-mm) pieces

½ tsp ground cinnamon

3 cups (750 g) plain Greek yogurt

¼ cup (30 g) walnuts, chopped

3 tbsp crystallized ginger, finely chopped

lime-infused nectarines, honey & granola

In a bowl, stir together the nectarines, honey, and lime zest. Divide half of the yogurt among 4 glasses, then layer on half of the fruit mixture. Top with the remaining yogurt and then the remaining fruit. Sprinkle with the granola and serve.

3 nectarines, halved, pitted, and sliced

2 tsp honey

Grated zest of 1 lime

3 cups (750 g) plain Greek yogurt

½ cup (60 g) granola

WHOLE-GRAIN BREAKFAST TOASTS

These inspired toasts are piled high with flavorful ingredients that will keep you satisfied every day of the week. Use the best-quality whole-grain bread you can find. Try a crusty whole-grain batard, walnut bread, or sliced multi-grain. Each recipe makes four toasts—enough to serve two or four.

avocado toasts with watercress, sunflower seeds & flaky sea salt

Top each toast with the avocado slices, slightly overlapping, and dividing them evenly. In a small bowl, toss the watercress with the olive oil and lemon juice and pile high on top of the avocados. Sprinkle with the sunflower seeds and salt, and serve.

4 slices whole-grain bread, toasted

1½ avocados, pitted, peeled, and thinly sliced

1½ cups (45 g) watercress, tough stems removed

2 tbsp extra-virgin olive oil

4 tsp fresh lemon juice

2 tbsp roasted unsalted sunflower seeds

Flaky sea salt, such as Maldon

smoked salmon toasts with dill cream cheese, red onion & capers

In a small bowl, stir together the cream cheese, dill, and lemon juice, and season to taste with salt and pepper. Spread the cream cheese mixture on the toasts, dividing it evenly. Top with the smoked salmon, red onion, capers, and chives and serve.

6 oz (185 g) cream cheese, at room temperature

2 tbsp chopped fresh dill

1 tsp fresh lemon juice

Salt and freshly ground pepper

4 slices whole-grain bread, toasted

¼ lb (125 g) thinly sliced smoked salmon

¼ cup (30 g) thinly sliced red onion

2 tbsp capers

1 tbsp finely chopped fresh chives

kabocha squash toasts with goat cheese & pepitas

Preheat the oven to 450°F (230°C). Line a baking sheet with parchment paper. Place the squash on the baking sheet, toss with 2 tbsp of the olive oil, and spread in a single layer. Season generously with salt and black pepper. Roast, stirring once, until soft and caramelized, 25–30 minutes.

In a frying pan, warm the remaining 1 tbsp olive oil over medium-high heat. Add the onion and cook, stirring occasionally, until softened, about 5 minutes. Add the red pepper flakes and cook, stirring occasionally, for 1 minute. Add the squash and stir to combine. Using a potato masher or a large fork, mash the squash mixture.

Spread the cheese on the toasts, dividing it evenly. Top with the squash mixture and sprinkle with the pepitas. Sprinkle with shichimi togarashi or drizzle with chili oil to taste, and serve.

½ kabocha squash, seeded, peeled, and cut into ½-inch (12-mm) pieces

3 tbsp olive oil

Salt and freshly ground black pepper

½ yellow onion, chopped

1 tsp red pepper flakes

¼ lb (125 g) fresh goat cheese, at room temperature

4 slices whole-grain bread, toasted

2 tbsp toasted pepitas

Shichimi togarashi or chili oil for garnish

cucumber toasts with radishes & sprouts

In a small bowl, stir together the cream cheese, feta cheese, green onion, and garlic, and season to taste with salt and pepper. Spread the cream cheese mixture on the toasts, dividing it evenly. Top with the cucumber, radishes, and sprouts. Season with salt and pepper and serve.

4 oz (125 g) cream cheese, at room temperature

2 oz (60 g) feta cheese, at room temperature

2 tbsp thinly sliced green onion

½ tsp minced garlic

Salt and freshly ground pepper

4 slices whole-grain bread, toasted

½ English cucumber, thinly sliced

2 radishes, thinly sliced

¼ cup (10 g) alfalfa sprouts or other sprouts

AVOCADO + WATERCRESS
+ SUNFLOWER SEEDS
+ FLAKY SEA SALT

SMOKED SALMON +
DILL CREAM CHEESE + RED ONION
+ CAPERS + CHIVES

SLICED CUCUMBER +
SHAVED RADISH + FETA–CREAM
CHEESE + SPROUTS

KABOCHA SQUASH + GOAT CHEESE
+ TOASTED PEPITAS
+ SHICHIMI TOGARASHI

FRESH FRUIT SMOOTHIE BOWLS

Smoothie bowls are all about customizing and accessorizing. The best ones are topped with something crunchy, something sweet, and plenty of fresh fruit. Arrange the fruit in beautifully composed bowls, or sprinkle on the toppings with haphazard abandon. Use the toppings suggested below or experiment with your own combinations. Each of the recipes makes enough for two meal-size bowls.

açai smoothie bowl

In a blender, combine the berry purée, raspberries, and coconut water and blend until smooth. Place in the freezer until chilled, about 20 minutes. Spoon the smoothie into two shallow bowls, dividing it evenly. Arrange the banana, strawberries, granola, and goji berries in rows on top. Sprinkle with the coconut, drizzle with the honey, and serve.

4 packets (3 oz/90 g each) frozen açai berry purée

¼ cup (60 g) frozen raspberries

½ cup (120 ml) coconut water or apple juice

1 banana, sliced

6 strawberries, stemmed, cored, and sliced

⅓ cup (45 g) granola

2 tbsp dried goji berries

2 tbsp shredded dried unsweetened coconut

1 tbsp honey

tropical smoothie bowl

In a blender, combine the yogurt, frozen strawberries, and 2 of the bananas and blend until smooth. Spoon the smoothie into two shallow bowls, dividing it evenly. Arrange the remaining banana, the mango, pineapple, and sliced strawberries on top. Sprinkle with the coconut and serve.

2 cups (500 g) plain Greek yogurt

1 cup (125 g) frozen strawberries or frozen diced mango

3 bananas, sliced

½ mango, pitted, peeled, and chopped

¾ cup (140 g) diced pineapple

6 strawberries, sliced

2 tbsp toasted unsweetened flaked coconut

protein smoothie bowl

In a blender, combine the yogurt, bananas, and almond butter and blend until smooth. Spoon the smoothie into two shallow bowls, dividing it evenly. Arrange the raspberries, almonds, and granola on top. Sprinkle with the cacao nibs and puffed brown rice and serve.

2 cups (500 g) plain Greek yogurt

2 bananas, sliced and frozen

3 tbsp almond butter

1 cup (120 g) raspberries

2 tbsp toasted almonds

2 tbsp chia granola

1 tbsp cacao nibs

1 tbsp puffed brown rice

green smoothie bowl

In a blender, combine the yogurt, avocado, spinach, bananas, and almond butter and blend until smooth. Spoon the smoothie into two shallow bowls, dividing it evenly. Arrange the mango and blueberries on top. Sprinkle with the pepitas and oat bran, and serve.

1 cup (250 g) plain Greek yogurt

½ avocado, pitted and peeled

2 cups (60 g) spinach leaves

2 frozen bananas

2½ tbsp almond butter

1 mango, peeled and sliced

½ pint (150 g) blueberries

1 tbsp toasted pepitas

1 tbsp toasted oat bran

mixed fruit smoothie bowl

In a blender, combine the almond milk, coconut milk, yogurt, banana, berries, and honey and blend until smooth. Taste and add more honey if desired. Spoon the smoothie into two shallow bowls, dividing it evenly. Arrange the raspberries and pomegranate seeds on top. Sprinkle with the coconut and wheat germ, and serve.

1 cup (240 ml) almond milk

1 cup (240 ml) coconut milk

1 cup (250 g) plain Greek yogurt

1 very ripe banana, peeled and frozen

1 cup (120 g) frozen mixed berries

2 tbsp honey, plus more to taste

¼ cup (30 g) fresh raspberries

2 tbsp pomegranate seeds

1 tbsp shredded dried unsweetened coconut

1 tbsp toasted wheat germ

START YOUR DAY BRIGHT

A thick mix of fresh fruit blended with Greek yogurt or coconut milk (or both) makes a rich, creamy, and intensely flavorful base for an artistic array of fruits, nuts, seeds, and grains.

AÇAI SMOOTHIE BOWL
with strawberries, banana, granola, coconut & goji berries

TROPICAL SMOOTHIE BOWL
with mango, pineapple, bananas, strawberries & toasted flaked coconut

PROTEIN SMOOTHIE BOWL
with almonds, raspberries, puffed brown rice & cacao nibs

MIXED FRUIT SMOOTHIE BOWL with raspberries, pomegranate seeds, coconut & toasted wheat germ

GREEN SMOOTHIE BOWL with mango, blueberries, pepitas & toasted oat bran

AÇAI SMOOTHIE BOWL with fresh cherries, granola, flaxseeds & chia seeds

SPICED HONEY BROILED GRAPEFRUIT

SERVES 6

Honey and the heat of the broiler give these grapefruit halves a crisp crown. For easy eating, use a serrated knife to cut alongside the membranes to loosen the segments.

3 grapefruits, halved and cut alongside each membrane (see note)

3 tbsp honey

1 tsp pure vanilla extract

1 pinch *each* **ground cardamom and ground cinnamon**

Preheat the broiler. Line a baking sheet with aluminum foil. In a small bowl, stir together the honey, vanilla, cardamom, and cinnamon.

Place the grapefruit halves, cut side up, on the prepared baking sheet. Drizzle each half with the honey mixture. Broil until bubbling, 2–3 minutes. Transfer to bowls or a platter and serve.

CINNAMON-BAKED APPLES

SERVES 8

Apples are brushed with cream and then rolled in sugar to create an appealing crisp crust in the oven. Serve them topped with a dollop of the leftover cream, if you like.

8 large Rome Beauty apples

1¼ cups (250 g) sugar

2 cups (500 ml) heavy cream

Ground cinnamon for sprinkling

Preheat the oven to 300°F (150°C). Use an apple corer to remove the apple cores. Place the sugar in a shallow bowl. Pour ⅓ cup (80 ml) of the cream into another small bowl. Dip a pastry brush into the bowl of cream and brush the outside of each apple, then roll the apples in the sugar to coat them completely.

Place the apples, stem side up, in a baking dish and sprinkle with cinnamon. Spoon the sugar and cream remaining in the bowls into the hollow cores of the apples, dividing evenly. Pour ½ cup (125 ml) water into the bottom of the baking dish. Bake, basting occasionally with the pan liquid, until tender, about 1½ hours. Serve warm or at room temperature. Whip the remaining cream to soft peaks and pass at the table.

NUT & SEED POWER BARS

MAKES 8 BARS

Rich in protein, essential nutrients, and antioxidants, these chewy granola bars will energize your day. A mix of oats, almonds, and seeds combines with a sweet-sticky blend of mashed dates and maple syrup to form a dense loaf from which bars may be cut. Mashing the dates well will help to hold the baked bars together. When baking, let the oats turn dark brown for the best flavor.

Canola oil for greasing

2 cups (185 g) rolled oats

½ cup (75 g) raw almonds, coarsely chopped

½ cup (60 g) raw pepitas

½ cup (60 g) raw sunflower seeds

2 tbsp flaxseeds

½ tsp salt

¾ cup (230 ml) dark maple syrup

6 Medjool dates, pitted and chopped

2 tbsp coconut oil

Preheat the oven to 350°F (180°C). Grease an 8-inch (20-cm) square baking pan with canola oil. Line the pan with parchment paper, allowing the paper to overhang the edge on two opposite sides, and grease the paper inside the pan.

In a large bowl, stir together the oats, almonds, pepitas, sunflower seeds, flaxseeds, and salt. Set aside.

In a small saucepan, combine the maple syrup and dates. Bring to a boil over medium-high heat. Reduce the heat and boil gently, stirring occasionally, until the dates are soft and the syrup is slightly thickened, 8–10 minutes.

Remove from the heat and, using a fork, mix in the coconut oil and mash the dates until the syrup is pulpy, about 2 minutes; you should have about 1 cup (345 g) syrup. Add the syrup to the oat mixture and stir with a rubber spatula until well coated. Spread the mixture in the prepared pan, using the back of the spatula to firmly press it into an even 1-inch (2.5-cm) layer.

Bake the bar slab until the top is dark brown and the mixture is firm around the edges and yields only slightly when pressed with your finger in the center, about 50 minutes. Let cool in the pan on a wire rack for 1 hour, then turn the bar slab out onto the rack and let cool completely. Using a serrated knife, cut into 8 bars. The bars can be wrapped in aluminum foil and stored at room temperature for up to 5 days.

EGGS

POACHED, FRIED, SCRAMBLED, BAKED,
OMELETS, FRITTATAS, STRATA & MORE

HARD-BOILED EGGS should have yolks that are creamy, not dry, and whites that are tender, not rubbery.

FRIED EGGS should be cooked over gentle heat to preserve nutrients and allow for even cooking.

MASTERING STOVE-TOP EGGS

Learning how to cook eggs is one of the essential skills to perfect when it comes to preparing breakfast.

POACHED EGGS cook easily in 2 inches (5 cm) of simmering water.

SCRAMBLED EGGS cook best in a nonstick skillet over medium-low heat until soft and creamy.

PERFECT EGGS

The unassuming egg is a miracle of biological engineering: the perfect package of protein, flavor, and versatility. Cooking eggs to perfection can have as much to do with personal preference as it can with technique. Learn the best methods, then modify them to suit your taste. Most recipes in this chapter (and the simple procedures here) allow for two eggs per person, but you can vary the number to cook as many or as few as you like.

hard-boiled

Place the eggs in a saucepan and cover with cold water by 2 inches (5 cm). Bring to a boil over medium-high heat. When the water comes to a boil, cover the pan, remove from the heat, and let the eggs stand in the water for 12 minutes. Drain the eggs and rinse under cold running water until cool. When the eggs are cool, crack and peel them.

8 large eggs

fried

To prepare sunny-side-up eggs, in a large frying pan, preferably nonstick, heat 1 tbsp of the olive oil over medium heat. Crack 4 of the eggs into the pan. Season with salt and pepper and cook until the whites are opaque and the yolks thicken, 2–3 minutes. Repeat with the remaining 1 tbsp olive oil and 4 eggs. Transfer to a plate and serve, or keep warm until all are cooked.

2 tbsp olive oil or unsalted butter
8 large eggs
Salt and freshly ground pepper

To prepare over-easy, over-medium, or over-hard eggs, cook as directed (above), then carefully flip the eggs with a nonstick spatula and cook for about 30 seconds longer for eggs over easy, about 1 minute longer for eggs over medium, and about 1½ minutes longer for eggs over hard.

Note: Start with cold eggs directly from the refrigerator. The yolks are more likely to stay intact when you crack the eggs.

poached

Pour water to a depth of 2 inches (5 cm) into a large, deep sauté pan. Bring to a gentle simmer over medium-low heat. One at a time, crack the eggs into a ramekin or a small cup and gently slide into the simmering water. Cook as many eggs at a time as will comfortably fit in the pan. Cook until the whites begin to set, about 2 minutes, then gently turn the eggs with a slotted spoon. Continue to cook until the whites are opaque and fully cooked and the yolks are still runny, about 2 minutes longer.

Using the slotted spoon, lift each egg from the simmering water, draining well. Blot the bottom of each egg briefly on a paper towel and serve, or keep warm until all are cooked.

8 large eggs

scrambled

In a bowl, whisk the eggs with the milk and season with salt and pepper. In a large nonstick frying pan, melt the butter over medium-low heat. Pour in the egg mixture and cook without stirring for 1 minute. Using a rubber spatula, gently stir the eggs, allowing the uncooked eggs to run to the bottom of the pan. Cook, stirring often, until the eggs are set but still creamy, about 4 minutes.

8 large eggs
2 tbsp whole milk
Salt and freshly ground pepper
2 tbsp unsalted butter

Make the hollandaise sauce first, transfer it to a bowl, and keep it warm in a larger bowl of hot water while you cook the eggs and bacon.

EGGS BLACKSTONE

SERVES 4

Buttery, lemony hollandaise sauce adds the finishing touch to this tomato-and-bacon-bedecked cousin of a classic eggs Benedict. Poaching eggs isn't difficult if you follow the basic method (below).

4 tomatoes, thickly sliced

1 tbsp olive oil

1 tsp minced fresh thyme

Salt and freshly ground pepper

8 slices thick-cut applewood-smoked bacon

8 slices coarse country bread

8 large eggs

1½ cups (350 ml) Hollandaise Sauce (page 120)

Preheat the oven to 400°F (200°C). Lightly grease a rimmed baking sheet. Arrange the tomatoes, cut side up, on the baking sheet. Drizzle with the oil, then sprinkle with the thyme, ½ teaspoon salt, and ¼ teaspoon pepper. Bake until the tomatoes have shrunk slightly and their juices are bubbling, about 30 minutes.

Meanwhile, fry the bacon, and toast and butter the bread. Set aside.

Pour water to a depth of 2 inches (5 cm) into a large, deep sauté pan. Bring to a gentle simmer over medium-low heat. One at a time, crack the eggs into a ramekin or a small cup and gently slide into the simmering water. Cook as many eggs at a time as will comfortably fit in the pan. Cook until the whites begin to set, about 2 minutes, then gently turn the eggs with a slotted spoon. Continue to cook until the whites are opaque and fully cooked and the yolks are still runny, about 2 minutes longer. Using the slotted spoon, lift each egg from the water and transfer to a paper towel–lined plate while you cook the remaining eggs.

Place 2 pieces of toast on each plate. Top each piece with 2 slices of tomato, 2 pieces of bacon, a warm egg, and a generous spoonful of the warm hollandaise sauce. Season with salt and pepper and serve.

VARIATIONS

Eggs Benedict

Omit the tomatoes. Substitute 8 slices fried Canadian bacon for the smoked bacon and 4 split, toasted, and buttered English muffins for the country bread. Place 1 slice of Canadian bacon on each muffin half, place a poached egg over the bacon, then top with hollandaise.

Eggs Florentine

Omit the tomatoes. Substitute 4 split, toasted, and buttered English muffins for the country bread. Instead of the smoked bacon, place about ¼ cup (7 g) firmly packed baby spinach leaves on each muffin half before adding the eggs and the hollandaise.

STEAK & EGGS WITH CHERRY TOMATOES

SERVES 4

A thick, juicy steak served alongside fried eggs for breakfast will stave off hunger for most of the day. A rib eye is a common choice, but a sirloin, strip, or even T-bone steak will do. Here, a vibrant sauté of cherry tomatoes brightens the classic duo. Serve with toasted English muffins to soak up the juices.

4 tbsp (60 ml) olive oil

4 small boneless beef rib-eye or top loin steaks, each about ½ inch (12 mm) thick

Salt and freshly ground pepper

1½ cups (280 g) cherry tomatoes, halved

1 tsp chopped fresh chives

½ tsp minced fresh thyme

8 large eggs

In a large heavy frying pan, preferably cast iron, warm 1 tbsp of the olive oil over medium-high heat until very hot. Trim the steaks of any surface fat and season with ½ tsp salt and ¼ tsp pepper. Add the steaks to the pan and cook until the undersides are nicely browned, about 3 minutes. Turn and cook until the other sides are browned, about 3 minutes longer for medium-rare. Transfer the steaks to a plate and tent with aluminum foil.

In the same pan, warm 2 tbsp olive oil over medium-high heat. Add the cherry tomatoes, ¼ tsp salt, and ⅛ tsp pepper. Cook, stirring frequently, just until the tomatoes begin to soften and release their juices, about 3 minutes. Stir in the chives and thyme.

In another large frying pan, warm the remaining 1 tbsp olive oil over medium heat. Crack 4 of the eggs into the pan. Season with salt and pepper, cover, reduce the heat to medium-low, and cook until the whites are opaque and the yolks thicken, 2–3 minutes. Or carefully flip the eggs and cook to the desired doneness. Repeat with the remaining eggs.

Place a steak and 2 fried eggs on each of 4 plates, top with the cherry tomatoes, and serve.

CORNED BEEF HASH WITH ONION & CHILE

SERVES 6

The secret to this satisfying breakfast hash is marrying chunky pieces of well-seasoned meat and potatoes with sweet, mellow caramelized onions and custardy soft-cooked eggs. A heavy frying pan, preferably cast iron, and a gentle press with spatula while frying will guarantee a crisp crust.

1 corned beef brisket, about 2⅓ lb (1.2 kg)

1 tsp *each* whole cloves, mustard seeds, black peppercorns, and coriander seeds

2 bay leaves

1 large russet potato, about ¾ lb (375 g), scrubbed

2 tbsp olive oil

1 small yellow onion, chopped

1 poblano chile, seeded and chopped

Salt and freshly ground pepper

2 tbsp unsalted butter

12 poached or fried eggs (pages 32–33)

Rinse the corned beef and put it in a large Dutch oven or a heavy pot. Add enough cold water to cover by 1 inch (2.5 cm). Bring to a boil over medium-high heat, skimming off any foam that rises to the surface. Add the cloves, mustard seeds, peppercorns, coriander seeds, and bay leaves. Reduce the heat to medium-low, cover, and simmer gently until almost tender, 2½–3 hours.

Add the potato to the pot and return the liquid to a simmer. Cook, uncovered, until the brisket and potato are fully tender, about 30 minutes longer. Transfer the corned beef and potato to a carving board and let cool completely. (The corned beef and potato can be cooled, covered, and refrigerated for up to 1 day.)

Slice the corned beef across the grain, trimming any excess fat. Coarsely chop enough corned beef to measure 2½ cups (470 g). Save the remaining corned beef for another use. Peel and shred the potato. Transfer the corned beef and potato to a food processor and pulse until finely chopped.

Meanwhile, in a large heavy frying pan, warm 1 tbsp of the olive oil over medium-low heat. Add the onion and cook, stirring often, until golden brown, 15–20 minutes. Transfer the onion to a bowl.

In the same pan, warm the remaining 1 tbsp olive oil over medium heat. Add the chile, cover, and cook, uncovering to stir occasionally, until tender, about 6 minutes. Add the chile and cooked onion to the beef mixture and stir to combine. Season to taste with salt and pepper.

In the same pan, melt the butter over medium heat. Divide the corned beef mixture into 6 portions and shape each portion into a thick patty. Place the patties in the pan and press gently with a metal spatula. Cook until the undersides are crisp and browned, about 5 minutes. Turn the patties over, press gently with the spatula, and cook until the other sides are browned, about 5 minutes longer.

Meanwhile, prepare the poached or fried eggs as directed and keep warm. Place each patty on a plate or in a shallow bowl, top with 2 poached or fried eggs, and serve.

SPICY ALL-VEGGIE HASH

SERVES 4–6

Fragrant and flavorful, this hearty egg-topped hash features two types
of roasted potatoes and a cumin-spiced sauté of onion, bell pepper,
chile, and corn. A last-minute sprinkling of fresh cilantro, followed
by a squeeze of fresh lime juice, adds depth to the dish.

2 tbsp olive oil, plus more
for greasing

1½ lb (680 g) orange-fleshed
sweet potatoes, peeled and
cut into small cubes

1½ lb (680 g) Yukon gold potatoes,
peeled and cut into small cubes

1 yellow onion, chopped

1 red bell pepper, seeded and
chopped

1 jalapeño chile, seeded and minced

8–12 poached or fried eggs (pages 32–33)

1 cup (185 g) fresh or thawed frozen
corn kernels

1½ tsp ground cumin

3 tbsp chopped fresh cilantro,
plus more for garnish

Salt and freshly ground pepper

Lime wedges for serving

Preheat the oven to 400°F (200°C). Lightly grease a large, rimmed baking sheet. Combine all of the potatoes on the prepared baking sheet, toss with 1 tbsp of the olive oil, and spread in a single layer. Roast for 30 minutes. Using a metal spatula, turn the potatoes and continue to roast until lightly browned and tender, about 15 minutes longer. Keep warm.

Meanwhile, in a large frying pan, warm the remaining 1 tbsp olive oil over medium heat. Add the onion, bell pepper, and jalapeño and cook, stirring occasionally, until the vegetables are tender, about 10 minutes. Meanwhile, prepare the poached or fried eggs as directed, cooking 1 or 2 per person, and keep warm.

Stir the corn into the hash mixture and cook until heated through, about 3 minutes. Stir in the cumin and cook until fragrant, about 30 seconds. Add all of the potatoes and the cilantro and stir to combine. Season to taste with salt and pepper.

Divide the hash among individual bowls. Top each serving with 1–2 poached or fried eggs and sprinkle with cilantro. Serve with lime wedges.

Poached eggs atop generous chunks of potatoes, onions, and peppers provide ample fuel for a full day.

OVEN-BAKED FRITTATAS

A frittata is essentially a crustless quiche and takes well to endless variations, such as these cheese- and vegetable-laden favorites. The basic method is the same for all: prepare the flavorings in a frying pan, add eggs beaten with a little milk (and sometimes cheese), and bake until firm. Each of these recipes serves five or six people.

herbed frittata with cherry tomatoes

Preheat the oven to 400°F (200°C).

In a large bowl, beat the eggs with the milk. Stir in the basil, parsley, mint, and chives. Season with salt and pepper. In an ovenproof frying pan, melt the butter over medium-high heat. Pour the egg mixture into the pan, sprinkle with the cheese and tomatoes, and cook without stirring for 2 minutes. Transfer the pan to the oven and bake until the eggs are set and the frittata is golden brown, 10–12 minutes. Loosen the edges with a rubber spatula, invert the frittata onto a platter, and cut into wedges.

In a large bowl, whisk together the olive oil and lemon juice, and season with salt and pepper. Add the arugula and toss to coat. Pile the salad on top of the frittata and serve.

10 large eggs

1 tbsp whole milk

1 tbsp *each* chopped fresh basil and chopped fresh flat-leaf parsley

1 tsp *each* chopped fresh mint and chopped fresh chives

Salt and freshly ground pepper

2 tbsp unsalted butter

¼ cup (30 g) shredded Gruyère cheese

½ cup (90 g) cherry tomatoes, halved

1½ tbsp olive oil

1½ tbsp fresh lemon juice

3 cups (90 g) arugula

egg white frittata with beet greens

Preheat the oven to 375°F (190°C).

In an ovenproof frying pan, warm the olive oil over medium-high heat. Add the onion and cook, stirring often, until softened, about 6 minutes. Add the beet greens, season with salt and pepper, and cook, stirring often, until wilted, about 2 minutes. Stir in the sun-dried tomatoes. Spread into an even layer. In a large bowl, whisk the egg whites and season with salt and pepper. Pour the egg whites into the pan and cook without stirring for 2 minutes, then sprinkle with the cheese. Transfer the pan to the oven and bake until the eggs are set, about 10 minutes. Loosen the edges with a rubber spatula. Invert the frittata onto a platter, cut into wedges, and serve.

2 tbsp olive oil

½ yellow onion, chopped

2 cups (100 g) packed beet greens, roughly chopped

Salt and freshly ground pepper

⅓ cup (75 g) oil-packed sun-dried tomatoes, drained and chopped

10 large egg whites

2 oz (60 g) feta cheese, crumbled

potato, onion & bacon frittata

Preheat the oven to 400°F (200°C).

In an ovenproof frying pan, cook the bacon over medium-high heat, turning once, until crispy, about 7 minutes. Let drain on paper towels, then tear into bite-size pieces.

Pour off all but 1 tbsp of the fat in the pan and return to medium-high heat. Add the olive oil and the potatoes. Season with salt and pepper and cook, stirring often, until the potatoes are fork-tender and golden around the edges, about 8 minutes. Add the green onions, garlic, rosemary, and cooked bacon. Cook, stirring occasionally, for 1 minute longer, and spread into an even layer. Stir the cheese into the egg mixture and add to the frying pan. Cook without stirring for 2 minutes. Transfer the pan to the oven and bake until the eggs are set and the frittata is golden brown, 10–12 minutes. Loosen the edges with a rubber spatula and carefully invert the frittata onto a platter. Cut into wedges and serve.

3 slices thick-cut bacon

1 tbsp olive oil

½ lb (250 g) fingerling potatoes, thinly sliced lengthwise

Salt and freshly ground pepper

3 green onions, sliced

2 cloves garlic, chopped

1 tbsp chopped fresh rosemary

3 tbsp grated pecorino cheese

10 large eggs beaten with 1 tbsp whole milk

asparagus & prosciutto frittata

Preheat the oven to 400°F (200°C).

Bring a saucepan of salted water to a boil over high heat. Add the asparagus and cook for 1 minute. Drain and set aside.

In an ovenproof frying pan, warm the olive oil over medium-high heat. Add the onion, season with salt and pepper, and cook, stirring often, until softened, about 6 minutes. Add the garlic and cook for 1 minute longer. Add the cooked asparagus and the prosciutto and spread into an even layer. Stir the cheese into the egg mixture and add to the frying pan. Cook without stirring for 2 minutes. Transfer the pan to the oven and bake until the eggs are set and the frittata is golden brown, 10–12 minutes. Loosen the edges with a rubber spatula and carefully invert the frittata onto a platter. Cut into wedges and serve.

Salt and freshly ground pepper

½ lb (250 g) asparagus, tough ends snapped off, spears cut into 2-inch (5-cm) pieces

2 tbsp olive oil

½ yellow onion, chopped

2 cloves garlic, chopped

3 slices prosciutto, coarsely chopped

3 tbsp grated Parmesan cheese

10 large eggs beaten with 1 tbsp whole milk

Experiment with your own favorite fillings. Try sautéed mushrooms, steamed asparagus, and a mix of good-quality cheeses.

CALIFORNIA OMELET

SERVES 2

With a little practice and a high-quality nonstick frying pan, making omelets can become an easy morning ritual. The best fillings start with a good melting cheese.

FOR THE FILLING

¼ cup (30 g) shredded Cheddar cheese

¼ cup (30 g) shredded Monterey jack cheese

3 slices thick-cut bacon, cooked and torn into bite-size pieces

½ avocado, pitted, peeled, and sliced

¼ cup (60 g) fresh salsa

¼ cup (15 g) packed alfalfa or sunflower sprouts

FOR THE OMELETS

4 large eggs

2 tbsp heavy cream

Salt and freshly ground pepper

½ tbsp unsalted butter

Assemble all of ingredients for the omelet filling. Set aside.

To make the omelets, in a bowl, whisk together the eggs, cream, ¼ tsp salt, and a few grinds of pepper just until blended. In a small frying pan, preferably nonstick, melt the butter over medium heat, tilting the pan to cover the bottom evenly with butter. Pour half of the egg mixture into the pan and cook until the eggs have barely begun to set around the edges, about 30 seconds. Using a heatproof spatula, lift the cooked edges and gently push them toward the center, tilting the pan to allow the liquid egg on top to flow underneath, then cook for 30 seconds longer. Repeat this process, moving around the perimeter of the pan, until no liquid egg remains.

When the eggs are almost completely set but still slightly moist on top, sprinkle half of the cheeses over half of the omelet. Scatter half each of the bacon, avocado, salsa, and sprouts over the cheese. Using the spatula, fold the untopped half of the omelet over the filled half to create a half-moon shape. Let the omelet cook for 30 seconds longer, then slide it onto a serving plate. Keep warm. Repeat to make a second omelet in the same manner and serve.

VARIATION

Mushrooms with Fontina & Thyme
In a nonstick frying pan, melt 1 tbsp unsalted butter over medium heat. Add ¼ lb (125 g) sliced white or cremini mushrooms and cook, stirring occasionally, until the mushrooms begin to brown, about 6 minutes. Stir in ½ tsp thyme and season with salt and pepper. Transfer to a bowl and set aside, along with ½ cup (60 g) shredded fontina cheese. Whisk the egg mixture and cook the first omelet, adding half the cheese then half the filling as directed. Repeat to cook the second omelet.

OMELET SOUFFLÉ

SERVES 4

This puffy omelet achieves the dramatic rise of a soufflé but with much less stress for the cook. Enhance its light, pillowy quality by keeping the add-ins to a minimum. A little cheese and some fresh herbs are all it requires. Serve the soufflé hot from the oven, as it will deflate as it cools.

6 large eggs, separated

½ tsp salt

⅛ tsp freshly ground pepper

½ tbsp unsalted butter, melted

2 oz (60 g) goat cheese, crumbled

2 tbsp chopped fresh chives

Preheat the oven to 350°F (180°C).

In a medium bowl, using a wire whisk or an electric mixer, beat the egg whites until soft peaks form. In a large bowl, whisk together the egg yolks, salt, and pepper. Using a rubber spatula, gently stir one-fourth of the egg whites into the yolks and then fold in the remaining whites until no white streaks remain.

Coat an 8-inch (20-cm) ovenproof frying pan with the melted butter. Pour the egg mixture into the pan. Sprinkle with the cheese and chives, and season with salt and pepper. Bake until the eggs are golden, puffed, and cooked through, 10–12 minutes. Cut into slices and serve.

ASIAN NOODLE BOWL WITH POACHED EGG

SERVES 4

This savory Asian breakfast bowl is exceptionally versatile. Replace the udon with soba or buckwheat noodles or even spaghetti. Swap the poached eggs for fried ones, or move the noodles to the side of the pan and scramble the eggs, then incorporate them into the noodles as you would with fried rice.

1½ lb (680 g) fresh udon noodles

4 large eggs

4 slices thick-cut bacon

3 tbsp light soy sauce

2 tsp mirin

1 tsp sugar

Freshly ground pepper

3 green onions, dark and pale green parts only, chopped

Cook the udon noodles according to the package directions. Drain, rinse with cold, running water, then drain again. Set aside.

Pour water to a depth of 2 inches (5 cm) into a large, deep sauté pan and bring to a gentle simmer over medium-low heat. One at a time, crack the eggs into a ramekin or a small cup and gently slide into the simmering water. Cook as many eggs at a time as will comfortably fit in the pan. Cook until the whites begin to set, about 2 minutes, then gently turn the eggs with a slotted spoon. Continue to cook until the whites are opaque and fully cooked and the yolks are still runny, about 2 minutes longer. Using the slotted spoon, lift each egg from the simmering water and transfer it onto a paper towel–lined plate. Set aside.

In a large heavy frying pan, preferably cast iron, cook the bacon over medium heat, turning once, until crispy, about 8 minutes. Transfer to paper towels to drain. Pour off all but 1 tbsp of the fat in the pan and return to medium heat. Add the udon noodles and stir in the soy sauce, mirin, and sugar. Toss to coat the noodles in the sauce, raise the heat to medium-high, and cook until the sauce is slightly reduced, 1–2 minutes. Cut the bacon into pieces, add the bacon pieces to the noodles, and toss to mix. Remove the pan from the heat and season to taste with pepper.

Divide the udon noodles among bowls. Top each bowl with a poached egg, garnish with the green onions, and serve.

QUINOA, BUTTERNUT SQUASH & KALE BREAKFAST BOWL

SERVES 4

Packed with protein from the quinoa and egg and topped with vitamin-rich vegetables, this power breakfast has it all. Feel free to swap in grains like farro, barley, or brown rice, and try other seasonal vegetable combinations, such as asparagus and morels or caramelized red onion and spinach.

2 cups (280 g) butternut squash cubes (½-inch/12-mm cubes)

6 tbsp (90 ml) olive oil

Salt and freshly ground pepper

1 bunch kale, tough stems removed, leaves chopped

1 cup (180 g) quinoa

2 cloves garlic, chopped

4 large eggs

Preheat the oven to 425°F (220°C). Line a baking sheet with parchment paper.

Place the squash on the prepared baking sheet and toss with 2 tbsp of the olive oil. Spread in a single layer and season with salt and pepper. Roast, stirring once, until the squash begins to soften, about 20 minutes. Remove the baking sheet from the oven and stir in the kale. Continue to roast until the squash is tender and caramelized and the kale is wilted, 7–9 minutes longer. Set aside.

Meanwhile, in a saucepan, combine the quinoa and 2 cups (500 ml) water. Place over medium-high heat and bring to a boil. Cover, reduce the heat to medium-low, and simmer until the water is absorbed, about 15 minutes. Set aside.

In a frying pan, warm the remaining 4 tbsp olive oil over medium heat. Add the garlic and cook, stirring occasionally, until soft, about 1 minute. Stir in the cooked quinoa, season with salt and pepper, and keep warm over low heat.

Bring a large saucepan of water to a boil over medium-high heat. Gently lower the eggs into the water and cook for exactly 7 minutes for soft-boiled eggs. Drain the eggs and cool under running cold water for 30 seconds. Peel and halve the eggs.

Divide the quinoa among individual bowls and top with the squash-kale mixture and 2 egg halves. Season the eggs with salt and pepper and serve.

Red quinoa offers colorful contrast to the squash and kale in this bowl but does not vary in flavor from its golden cousin.

HUEVOS RANCHEROS

SERVES 4

Although this hearty dish of corn tortillas, fried eggs, beans, and ranchero sauce originated in rural Mexico, it has become popular breakfast fare throughout the United States. For a late-morning meal, accompany each serving with an icy cold Michelada (page 115) rimmed with chile-spiked salt.

FOR THE RANCHERO SAUCE

1 tbsp canola oil

1 small yellow onion, chopped

½ jalapeño chile, seeded and minced

2 cloves garlic, minced

1 can (14½ oz/415 g) diced tomatoes with juices

½ cup (125 ml) canned tomato sauce

1 tsp chili powder

1 canned chipotle pepper in adobo, chopped, plus ½ tsp adobo sauce (optional)

Salt and freshly ground pepper

4 tbsp (60 ml) olive oil

8 corn tortillas, each 6 inches (15 cm)

8 large eggs

Salt and freshly ground pepper

½ cup (75 g) crumbled queso fresco or feta cheese

Fresh cilantro leaves for garnish

Cooked black beans, warmed, for serving

To make the ranchero sauce, in a saucepan, warm the canola oil over medium heat. Add the onion, jalapeño, and garlic and cook, stirring occasionally, until softened, about 5 minutes. Transfer to a blender. Add the tomatoes and their juices, tomato sauce, chili powder, and chipotle pepper and adobo sauce (if using) and purée. Return the mixture to the saucepan and bring to a boil over high heat. Reduce the heat to medium-low and cook, stirring often, until reduced to about 2 cups (500 ml), about 30 minutes. Season to taste with salt and pepper. Cover and keep warm over low heat.

Preheat the oven to 200°F (95°C). Have ready 4 ovenproof plates.

In a frying pan, warm 2 tbsp of the olive oil over high heat. One at a time, fry the tortillas, turning once, just until crisp (they should not be crunchy), about 30 seconds. Transfer to paper towels to drain. Overlap 2 tortillas on each plate and keep warm in the oven. Discard the oil in the pan.

In the same pan, warm the remaining 2 tbsp olive oil over medium heat. Crack 4 of the eggs into the pan. Season with salt and pepper, cover, reduce the heat to medium-low, and cook until the whites are opaque and the yolks thicken, 2–3 minutes for sunny-side-up eggs. Or carefully flip the eggs and cook to the desired doneness. Transfer 2 eggs to each of 2 plates in the oven, placing them on the tortillas, and keep warm while frying the remaining eggs.

For each serving, spoon about ½ cup (125 ml) of the warm sauce over and around the eggs, top with one-fourth of the cheese, and sprinkle with cilantro. Pass the black beans at the table.

BREAKFAST BURRITOS

SERVES 4

A breakfast burrito doesn't claim to be fancy, but it's a favorite with kids and grown-ups alike. You can set out all the ingredients burrito-bar style and let everyone assemble their own. For a change, replace the chorizo with chicken-apple sausage, bacon, or shredded chicken, and swap in sweet potatoes for the russets.

2 russet potatoes, peeled

2 tbsp olive oil

Salt and freshly ground pepper

6 oz (185 g) fresh Mexican-style chorizo, casings removed

8 large eggs

2 tbsp whole milk

1 tbsp unsalted butter

4 large flour tortillas

1 can (15 oz/425 g) black beans, drained, rinsed, and warmed

½ cup (125 g) guacamole

½ cup (125 g) fresh salsa

Shred the potatoes. Wrap the potatoes in a kitchen towel and wring the towel to remove excess moisture.

In a large nonstick frying pan, warm 1½ tbsp of the olive oil over medium-high heat. Add the potatoes, season generously with salt and pepper, and drizzle with the remaining ½ tbsp olive oil. Fry the potatoes without stirring until golden brown underneath, about 6 minutes. Flip the potatoes and cook until golden brown on the second side, about 6 minutes. Transfer to a plate and cover loosely with aluminum foil.

Return the pan to medium-high heat, add the chorizo, and cook, breaking it up with a wooden spoon and stirring occasionally, until browned and cooked through, about 6 minutes. Transfer to a plate and cover loosely with aluminum foil. Discard the fat in the pan.

In a bowl, whisk the eggs with the milk and season with salt and pepper. In the same pan, melt the butter over medium-low heat. Pour in the eggs and cook without stirring for 1 minute. Using a rubber spatula, gently stir the eggs, allowing the uncooked eggs to run to the bottom of the pan, and cook until the eggs are set but still creamy, about 4 minutes.

Lay the tortillas on a work surface and fill each with one-fourth of the potatoes, chorizo, scrambled eggs, and black beans, leaving a 1-inch (2.5-cm) border on the ends. Fold two of the sides over and then roll up each burrito. Place the burritos, seam side down, on individual plates. Serve with the guacamole and salsa on the side.

For added flavor and texture, offer fresh pico de gallo for spooning over the tacos at the table.

BREAKFAST TACOS WITH PICKLED RED ONIONS & LIME-JALAPEÑO CREMA

SERVES 4

The tang of pickled red onions offers delicious contrast to fluffy scrambled eggs tucked into warm tortillas. The longer you let the onions sit, the tastier they will be. Use any leftover onions on sandwiches or in salads throughout the week.

⅓ cup (35 g) thinly sliced red onion

3 tbsp rice vinegar

½ tsp sugar

½ cup (125 g) sour cream or crème fraîche

1 tbsp fresh lime juice

1 tsp finely chopped seeded jalapeño chile

Salt and freshly ground pepper

8 large eggs

2 tbsp whole milk

2 tbsp unsalted butter

8 flour or corn tortillas, each 6 inches (15 cm), warmed

½ cup (105 g) canned pinto beans, drained, rinsed, and warmed

1 avocado, pitted, peeled, and sliced

½ cup (75 g) crumbled Cotija or feta cheese, or shredded Monterey jack

Fresh cilantro leaves for garnish

In a small nonaluminum bowl, stir together the onion, vinegar, and sugar. Let stand at room temperature for at least 30 minutes, or cover and refrigerate for up to 1 week.

In a small bowl, stir together the sour cream, lime juice, and jalapeño. Season to taste with salt and pepper. Let the crema stand at room temperature until serving, or cover and refrigerate for up to 3 days.

In a bowl, whisk the eggs with the milk and season with salt and pepper. In a large nonstick frying pan, melt the butter over medium-low heat. Pour in the eggs and cook without stirring for 1 minute. Using a rubber spatula, gently stir the eggs, allowing the uncooked eggs to run to the bottom of the pan, and cook until the eggs are set but still creamy, about 4 minutes.

Fill the tortillas with the scrambled eggs, pinto beans, avocado, cheese, and pickled onions. Drizzle with the crema, sprinkle with cilantro, and serve.

SHAKSHUKA WITH FETA & FARRO

SERVES 6

This North African dish features eggs poached in a spiced tomato sauce. In this variation, the sauce and eggs are spooned over bowls of farro, an ancient grain native to the Mediterranean region. While shakshuka doesn't traditionally include feta, the cheese provides a creamy counterpoint to the spices in the sauce.

2 tbsp olive oil

½ yellow onion, chopped

1 clove garlic, chopped

1 red bell pepper, roasted, seeded, peeled, and cut into ½-inch (12-mm) pieces, or about ½ cup (80 g) drained and diced bottled roasted red peppers

2 tsp ground cumin

¾ tsp smoked paprika

⅛ tsp red pepper flakes

Salt and freshly ground black pepper

1 can (28 oz/875 g) diced tomatoes with juices

¼ lb (125 g) feta cheese, crumbled

6 large eggs

3 cups (510 g) cooked farro

2 tbsp chopped fresh flat-leaf parsley

Preheat the oven to 350°F (180°C).

In a large ovenproof frying pan, warm the olive oil over medium-high heat. Add the onion and cook, stirring occasionally, until softened, about 6 minutes. Add the garlic and cook, stirring occasionally, for 1 minute. Stir in the bell pepper, cumin, paprika, and red pepper flakes. Season with salt and black pepper and cook, stirring occasionally, until fragrant, about 1 minute. Stir in the tomatoes and their juices and bring to a boil. Reduce the heat to low and simmer, stirring occasionally, until thickened, about 10 minutes. Season to taste with salt and black pepper.

Stir the cheese into the tomato sauce. Crack the eggs on top, spacing them evenly apart. Transfer the pan to the oven and bake until the egg whites are opaque, about 10 minutes.

Divide the farro evenly among 6 bowls. Top each with a poached egg and a generous portion of the sauce. Sprinkle evenly with the parsley and serve.

MEDITERRANEAN STRATA

SERVES 4–6

This version of the make-ahead breakfast favorite combines artichokes, olives, and sun-dried tomatoes with mozzarella and crusty bread. Be sure to let the assembled dish stand for at least one hour before baking so the bread will absorb the egg mixture, becoming more moist and tender.

1 tbsp unsalted butter

½ lb (250 g) crusty Italian bread, preferably day-old, cut into 1-inch (2.5-cm) cubes

1 can (14 oz/400 g) artichoke hearts, drained well and chopped

⅓ cup (45 g) Kalamata olives, pitted and halved

¼ cup (60 g) oil-packed sun-dried tomatoes, drained and sliced

¼ lb (125 g) mozzarella cheese, shredded

1½ tbsp grated Parmesan cheese

½ cup (15 g) lightly packed fresh basil leaves, chopped

6 large eggs

2 cups (500 ml) whole milk

Salt and freshly ground pepper

Butter the bottom and sides of a 9-by-13-inch (23-by-33-cm) baking dish that is 2 inches (5 cm) deep. Place the bread cubes in a single layer in the prepared dish. Top with the artichoke hearts, olives, sun-dried tomatoes, mozzarella, Parmesan, and basil, spreading the ingredients out evenly.

In a large bowl, whisk together the eggs and milk, and season with salt and pepper. Pour the egg mixture over the strata. Cover the dish with aluminum foil and let stand at room temperature for 1 hour, or refrigerate for up to 24 hours.

Preheat the oven to 375°F (190°C).

Bake the strata, covered, for 20 minutes. Uncover and continue to bake until the eggs are set and the strata is golden brown, about 20 minutes longer. Let cool slightly, then cut into squares and serve.

ASPARAGUS, CORN & EGG TART

SERVES 4–6

Salty with pancetta, creamy with melted cheese, and crunchy with corn and asparagus, this savory tart makes a delicious centerpiece for a weekend brunch. Seek out the thinnest asparagus spears you can find, or cut thick spears into thin diagonal slices. To save time, prepare the dough and line the pan a day in advance.

Cornmeal Tart Dough (page 123)

FOR THE FILLING

¼ lb (125 g) thin asparagus spears, ends trimmed

¼ lb (125 g) thinly sliced pancetta, diced

6 green onions, thinly sliced

3 cloves garlic, minced

1 cup (185 g) fresh or thawed frozen corn kernels

Freshly ground pepper

¼ lb (125 g) mozzarella or fontina cheese, shredded

¼ lb (125 g) Gruyère cheese, shredded

⅓ cup (80 ml) heavy cream

4–6 large eggs

½ cup (20 g) sunflower sprouts or pea shoots (optional)

Prepare the cornmeal tart dough, line the tart pan with the dough, and refrigerate as directed.

Preheat the oven to 375°F (190°C). Bake the tart shell just until set, about 12 minutes. Remove from the oven and let cool for 5–10 minutes.

Meanwhile, prepare the filling: Bring a sauté pan of water to a boil over high heat. Have ready a bowl of ice water. Add the asparagus to the boiling water and blanch just until bright but still crisp, 1–2 minutes. Using tongs, transfer the asparagus to the ice water to cool, then drain. Set aside.

In a frying pan, cook the pancetta over medium heat, stirring occasionally, until lightly browned, about 5 minutes. Add the onions and garlic and cook, stirring occasionally, until softened, about 2 minutes. If using fresh corn, add the kernels and stir until bright, about 30 seconds; if using thawed frozen corn, remove the pan from the heat, then stir in the corn. Season to taste with pepper.

Spread the pancetta mixture evenly over the tart shell. Sprinkle evenly with both cheeses, drizzle the cream over the cheese, and scatter the asparagus on top.

Bake the tart until the cheese has melted, about 10 minutes. Remove the tart from the oven and crack the eggs on top, spacing them evenly apart. Return the tart to the oven and continue to bake until the egg whites are opaque and the crust is golden, 12–14 minutes longer. Let the tart cool briefly, then remove the pan side. Just before serving, scatter the sprouts, if using, over the tart. Cut into individual pieces and serve warm or at room temperature.

GRILLED CHEDDAR SANDWICH WITH BACON, TOMATO & EGG

SERVES 4

A crisp, buttery exterior and a hot, melted interior are the hallmarks of a great grilled cheese sandwich. Add thick strips of bacon, generous slices of ripe tomato, and a just-fried egg, and the iconic sandwich becomes ideal morning fare. Swap out the Cheddar for Swiss, mozzarella, or fontina cheese, if you like.

8–12 slices thick-cut applewood-smoked bacon

6 tbsp (90 g) unsalted butter, at room temperature

4 large eggs

Salt and freshly ground pepper

8 slices coarse country bread

½ lb (250 g) sharp farmhouse Cheddar cheese, thinly sliced

8 thick slices ripe tomato, drained on paper towels

In a large frying pan, cook the bacon over medium heat, turning once, until crisp and brown, about 8 minutes. Transfer to paper towels to drain. Discard the fat in the pan. Rinse the pan with water and wipe clean with paper towels. Cut each bacon slice in half crosswise and set aside.

In the same pan, melt 2 tbsp of the butter over medium heat. Crack the eggs into the pan. Season with salt and pepper, cover, reduce the heat to medium-low, and cook until the whites are set and the yolks thicken, 2–3 minutes for sunny-side-up eggs. Or carefully flip the eggs and cook to the desired doneness.

Lay 4 of the bread slices on a work surface and top each with one-eighth of the cheese, 2 tomato slices, one-fourth of the bacon, 1 egg, and the remaining cheese. Cover with the remaining bread slices. Spread the outsides of each sandwich with 1 tbsp of the remaining butter.

Return the frying pan to medium heat or preheat an electric panini press according to the manufacturer's directions. Add the sandwiches. Place a flat lid or a heatproof plate on top of the sandwiches in the frying pan to weight them down, or cover the press. Cook until golden brown, about 4 minutes total. (If using a frying pan, turn the sandwiches to cook both sides, weighting each side down to compress the sandwiches.) Cut the sandwiches in half and serve.

BREAKFAST BANH MI
WITH PICKLED VEGETABLES

SERVES 4

A classic Vietnamese street sandwich, banh mi is made with roast pork and accented with Sriracha mayonnaise, pickled vegetables, and fresh herbs. This riff replaces the pork with bacon for a quick breakfast sandwich. You can make the Sriracha mayonnaise and refrigerate it for up to a week in advance.

1 carrot, shredded

½ small red onion, halved and thinly sliced

¼ cup (60 ml) rice vinegar

1½ tsp sugar

Salt and freshly ground pepper

1 baguette

½ cup (125 ml) mayonnaise

2½ tbsp Sriracha

1½ tbsp fresh lemon juice

8 slices thick-cut bacon

4 large eggs

¼ cup (7 g) fresh cilantro leaves

2 tbsp fresh mint leaves

In a nonaluminum bowl, combine the carrot, onion, vinegar, sugar, and ½ tsp salt and stir to combine. Set aside at room temperature for at least 20 minutes or up to 2 hours, or cover and refrigerate for up to 5 days.

Cut the baguette crosswise into 4 equal pieces and split each in half horizontally. In a small bowl, stir together the mayonnaise, Sriracha, and lemon juice. Set aside at room temperature.

In a large frying pan, cook the bacon over medium-high heat, turning once, until crispy, about 7 minutes. Transfer to paper towels to drain. Pour off all but 1 tbsp of the fat in the pan.

Return the pan to medium heat. Crack the eggs into the pan. Season with salt and pepper, cover, reduce the heat to medium-low, and cook until the whites are set and the yolks thicken, 2–3 minutes for sunny-side-up eggs. Or carefully flip the eggs and cook to the desired doneness.

Drain the pickled vegetables and stir in the cilantro and mint. Spread the cut sides of the baguette pieces with the Sriracha mayonnaise. Add 2 bacon slices, pickled vegetables, and a fried egg to the bottom halves of each baguette piece. Cover with the top halves and serve.

ULTIMATE BREAKFAST SANDWICHES

Add a fried egg and some pork or bacon to your favorite hot sandwich and it becomes the best kind of breakfast food—rich, melty, and packed with flavor and protein.

BREAKFAST CUBANO features Swiss cheese, deli ham, pickles, and fried egg between slices of mustard-slathered bread.

GRILLED CHEDDAR SANDWICH tucks a fried egg between layers of sliced tomato, crisp bacon, and melted Cheddar.

BREAKFAST BANH MI combines the crunch of bacon and pickled veggies with the ooze of fried egg and Sriracha mayonnaise.

CROQUE MADAME is the egg-topped counterpart of its French relative, the croque monsieur.

BREAKFAST CUBANO

SERVES 4

In our easy breakfast version of the popular Cuban sandwich known as a cubano, we swap in thinly sliced deli ham and a just-fried egg for the traditional roast pork. But don't worry, we kept the traditional garnishes of yellow mustard, Swiss cheese, and sliced pickles. Why mess with a good thing?

8 slices crusty French or Italian bread, each ½ inch (12 mm) thick

⅓ cup (75 g) yellow mustard

8 slices Swiss cheese

6 oz (185 g) sliced ham

2 dill pickles, each cut lengthwise into 4 slices

5 tbsp (75 g) unsalted butter, at room temperature

4 large eggs

Spread one side of the bread slices generously with the mustard. Place a slice of cheese (folded in half if necessary) on each bread slice. Top 4 bread slices with 2 or 3 slices of ham, then top each of the remaining bread slices with 2 pickle slices. Set aside.

In a large frying pan, melt 2 tbsp of the butter over medium heat. Crack the eggs into the pan. Cover and cook, turning once, until the whites are set but the yolks are still partially runny, 3–4 minutes.

Place the eggs on the pickle-topped bread slices, then cover with the ham-topped bread slices. Spread some of the butter on the tops of the sandwiches. In the same frying pan, melt the remaining butter over medium heat. Add the sandwiches buttered side up to the pan, cover, and cook, turning once, until golden brown, about 4 minutes per side. Cut the sandwiches in half and serve.

HAM & GRUYÈRE CROQUE MADAME

SERVES 4

A croque madame is so much more than a grilled ham-and-cheese sandwich.
In signature French fashion, this otherwise humble staple of Paris café and bar menus
is drenched in a decadent cheese sauce, then broiled until bubbling and golden.
A fried egg on top distinguishes it from its equally famous sibling, the croque monsieur.

4 tbsp (60 g) unsalted butter

2 tbsp all-purpose flour

1 cup (240 ml) whole milk, warmed

1 cup (125 g) shredded Gruyère cheese

5 tsp Dijon mustard

Salt and freshly ground pepper

8 slices good-quality, firm white sandwich bread

4 large eggs

½ lb (250 g) thinly sliced Black Forest ham

In a small saucepan, melt 2 tbsp of the butter over medium-low heat. Whisk in the flour until smooth. Let bubble without browning, whisking frequently, for 1 minute. Gradually whisk in the warm milk, raise the heat to medium, and bring to a gentle boil, whisking frequently. Reduce the heat to medium-low and simmer, whisking frequently, until thickened, about 5 minutes. Remove from the heat. Stir in ¾ cup (90 g) of the cheese and 1 tsp of the mustard. Season to taste with salt and pepper. Transfer to a bowl, cover with a piece of plastic wrap pressed directly onto the surface of the sauce, and let cool.

Preheat the oven to 400°F (200°C). Line a rimmed baking sheet with parchment paper.

Arrange the bread slices in a single layer on the prepared baking sheet. Bake, turning once, until toasted on both sides, about 10 minutes. Set aside.

In a large frying pan, melt the remaining 2 tbsp butter over medium heat. Crack the eggs into the pan. Season with salt and pepper, cover, reduce the heat to medium-low, and cook until the whites are set and the yolks thicken, 2–3 minutes for sunny-side-up eggs. Or carefully flip the eggs and cook to the desired doneness.

Preheat the broiler.

Spread 4 bread slices with the remaining 4 tsp mustard, then add an equal amount of the sliced ham and 1 tbsp of the sauce to each slice. Cover with the remaining bread slices. Return the sandwiches to the baking sheet. Spread the remaining sauce over the tops of the sandwiches and sprinkle each with 1 tbsp of the remaining cheese. Broil until the cheese is melted and golden, about 2 minutes. Transfer to individual plates, top each with a fried egg, and serve.

Serve this dish
hot from the oven
with sturdy toasts
for scooping up
the soft–baked
eggs and spinach.

BAKED EGGS WITH PROSCIUTTO & SPINACH

SERVES 4

This simple egg recipe can be almost fully assembled a day in advance and then slipped into the oven just before it's time to eat. Simply fill the ramekins with the sautéed spinach, prosciutto, and cream and set them aside. Then about 20 minutes before serving, crack an egg into each ramekin, add a drizzle of cream, and bake.

1 tbsp unsalted butter, plus more for greasing

1½ lb (680 g) spinach, rinsed but not dried

1 tsp olive oil

3 oz (90 g) prosciutto, chopped

¾ cup (180 ml) heavy cream, plus 4 tsp

Salt and freshly ground pepper

Ground nutmeg

4 large eggs

4 tsp grated Parmesan cheese

Preheat the oven to 350°F (180°C). Butter four ¾-cup (180-ml) ramekins.

In a large saucepan, melt the 1 tbsp butter over medium heat. Add the spinach a handful at a time and cook until the first batch wilts before adding another handful. Cook all of the spinach until tender, about 3 minutes. Drain the spinach in a sieve, pressing gently to remove excess liquid. Transfer to a cutting board and coarsely chop.

In the same saucepan, warm the olive oil over medium heat. Add the prosciutto and cook, stirring occasionally, until the fat softens, about 2 minutes. Add the spinach and the ¾ cup (180 ml) cream and bring to a boil. Cook, stirring often, until the cream has thickened and reduced to a few tbsp, about 4 minutes. Season with salt, pepper, and nutmeg. Divide evenly among the prepared ramekins. Crack an egg into each ramekin. Season the eggs with salt and pepper and drizzle each with 1 tsp of the cream. Arrange the ramekins on a rimmed baking sheet.

Bake, watching the eggs carefully to avoid overcooking, until the whites are opaque and the yolks have firm edges and are soft in the center, about 15 minutes. Remove from the oven, sprinkle each serving with 1 tsp of the cheese, and serve.

SCRAMBLED EGGS MADE SPECIAL

Although preparing scrambled eggs is quite simple, these tips will ensure delicious success: Use a nonstick frying pan, lighten the beaten eggs with a few tablespoons of milk, cook the eggs over medium-low heat, stir them gently while cooking, and be sure to season well. Scrambled eggs are wonderful on their own, but add-ins can make them even better. Each recipe serves four.

cajun scrambled eggs

In a large nonstick frying pan, warm the olive oil over medium-high heat. Add the bell pepper and sausage and cook, stirring frequently, until the pepper is soft and the sausage is browned, about 5 minutes. Reduce the heat to medium-low and add the butter to the pan, swirling the pan until the butter melts. Season the egg mixture with salt and pepper and pour into the pan. Cook without stirring for 1 minute. Using a rubber spatula, gently stir the eggs, allowing the uncooked eggs to run to the bottom of the pan. Cook until the eggs are mostly set, about 3 minutes, then stir in the cheese and green onions. Continue to gently stir until the eggs are set, about 1 minute longer, and serve.

2 tbsp olive oil

½ red bell pepper, seeded and diced

6 oz (185 g) andouille sausage, halved lengthwise and sliced

1 tbsp unsalted butter

8 large eggs beaten with 2 tbsp whole milk

Salt and freshly ground pepper

¼ cup (30 g) shredded Monterey jack cheese

2 green onions, white and pale green parts, thinly sliced

smoked salmon, crème fraîche & chives scrambled eggs

In a large nonstick frying pan, melt the butter over medium-low heat. Season the egg mixture with salt and pepper and pour into the pan. Cook without stirring for 1 minute. Using a rubber spatula, gently stir the eggs, allowing the uncooked eggs to run to the bottom of the pan. Cook until the eggs are mostly set, about 3 minutes, then stir in the smoked salmon and chives. Continue to gently stir until the eggs are set, about 1 minute longer. Divide the eggs among 4 plates, top each with 2 tbsp of the crème fraîche, sprinkle with the lemon zest, and serve.

2 tbsp unsalted butter

8 large eggs beaten with 2 tbsp whole milk

Salt and freshly ground pepper

¼ lb (125 g) smoked salmon, chopped

2 tbsp chopped fresh chives

½ cup (125 g) crème fraîche, at room temperature

1 tbsp grated lemon zest

kielbasa, arugula & gouda scrambled eggs

In a large nonstick frying pan, warm the olive oil over medium-high heat. Add the shallot and kielbasa and cook, stirring frequently, until the shallot is softened and the kielbasa is browned, about 5 minutes. Reduce the heat to medium-low and add the butter to the pan, swirling the pan until the butter melts. Season the egg mixture with salt and pepper and pour into the pan. Cook without stirring for 1 minute. Using a rubber spatula, gently stir the eggs, allowing the uncooked eggs to run to the bottom of the pan. Cook until the eggs are mostly set, about 3 minutes, then stir in the cheese and arugula. Continue to gently stir until the eggs are set, about 1 minute longer, and serve.

2 tbsp olive oil

1 shallot, thinly sliced

6 oz (185 g) kielbasa, halved lengthwise and thinly sliced

8 large eggs beaten with 2 tbsp whole milk

Salt and freshly ground pepper

1 tbsp unsalted butter

¼ cup (30 g) shredded Gouda cheese

1 cup (30 g) packed arugula

dill & cream cheese scrambled eggs with tiny croutons

In a large nonstick frying pan, melt 1 tbsp of the butter with the olive oil over medium-high heat. Add the bread cubes and season generously with salt and pepper. Toast the bread, allowing it to sit for a minute at a time before stirring, until golden brown, about 4 minutes total. Transfer the croutons to a plate. Do not wipe out the pan.

In the same pan, melt the remaining 2 tbsp butter over medium-low heat. Season the egg mixture with salt and pepper and pour into the pan. Cook without stirring for 1 minute. Using a rubber spatula, gently stir the eggs, allowing the uncooked eggs to run to the bottom of the pan. Cook until the eggs are mostly set, about 3 minutes, then stir in the cream cheese and dill. Continue to gently stir until the eggs are set, about 1 minute longer. Divide the eggs among 4 plates, top with the croutons, and serve.

3 tbsp unsalted butter

1 tbsp olive oil

¾ cup (45 g) tiny (¼-inch/6-mm) cubes whole-grain crusty bread

Salt and freshly ground pepper

8 large eggs beaten with 2 tbsp whole milk

5 oz (155 g) cream cheese, cut into cubes, at room temperature

2 tbsp chopped fresh dill

HOMESTYLE FRIES

SERVES 6

A healthy stack of home fries does as much to enhance a plate of morning eggs as the routine addition of bacon slices or sausage links. Put the trio together—eggs, meat, potatoes—and you create a breakfast offering that's sure to satisfy.

Salt and freshly ground pepper

3 large Yukon gold potatoes, scrubbed

2 tbsp unsalted butter

1 tbsp olive oil

1 yellow onion, diced

1 small red bell pepper, seeded and diced

4 green onions, chopped

Bring a large pot of salted water to a boil over high heat. Add the potatoes and cook until tender when pierced with a small knife, about 35 minutes. Drain the potatoes and let cool, then refrigerate until cold, at least 2 hours or up to 1 day. Peel the potatoes and cut into ½-inch (12-mm) cubes.

In a large nonstick frying pan, melt the butter with the olive oil over medium-high heat. Add the potatoes, yellow onion, and bell pepper and toss to coat. Cook, stirring occasionally, until just browned, about 15 minutes. Sprinkle with 1 tsp salt and ½ tsp pepper and cook until golden brown, about 5 minutes longer. Transfer the fries to a serving bowl, sprinkle with the green onions, and serve.

For perfect bacon every time, lay slices on a flat wire rack set in a rimmed baking sheet. Bake at 400°F (200°C) for 15–20 minutes.

SHREDDED HASH BROWNS

SERVES 4

Here are the four steps to perfect hash browns: soak the grated potatoes in water to release their starch, squeeze the soaked strands dry to prevent sogginess, pan fry the potatoes undisturbed on the first side to develop a nice crust, then carefully flip the potatoes while keeping the "cake" whole to brown the second side.

1 tbsp unsalted butter	Salt and freshly ground pepper
1 yellow onion, chopped	3 large russet potatoes, about
1 green or red bell pepper, seeded and chopped	1½ lb (680 g) total, peeled
	4 tbsp (60 ml) canola oil

In a heavy frying pan, preferably cast iron, melt the butter over medium heat. Add the onion and bell pepper and cook, stirring occasionally, until tender, about 10 minutes. Season with salt and pepper. Transfer to a bowl.

Shred the potatoes. Line a colander with cheesecloth and set the colander in the sink or over a bowl. Transfer the potatoes to the colander and twist the cheesecloth tightly into a pouch, squeezing out the moisture. Let the potatoes drain for 15 minutes. Squeeze the cheesecloth again, then transfer the potatoes to a large bowl. Add 1½ tsp salt and ¼ tsp pepper and stir well.

In the same frying pan, warm 2 tbsp of the canola oil over medium-high heat. Add the potato mixture and spread into a thick cake. Reduce the heat to medium, cover, and cook until golden brown and crisp underneath, about 6 minutes. Using a wide metal spatula, slide the potato cake onto a plate. Warm the remaining 2 tbsp canola oil in the pan. Carefully flip the potato cake, browned side up, into the pan. Cook until golden brown and crisp on the second side, about 6 minutes.

Slide the potatoes onto a platter. Return the onion mixture to the pan and cook, stirring often, until heated through, about 1 minute. Heap the onion mixture onto the potatoes and serve.

BACON, LEEK & GRUYÈRE QUICHE

SERVES 6

This classic quiche, a variation of quiche Lorraine, marries complementary ingredients in a buttery tart crust. Bake the quiche in a single pan, or divide among four 4¾-inch (12-cm) tartlet pans and bake for 25 minutes. Swap out the bacon for ham and substitute Cheddar or fontina for the Gruyère, if you like.

Single-Crust Flaky Pie Dough (page 123)

All-purpose flour for dusting

4 slices thick-cut applewood-smoked bacon, coarsely chopped

1 tbsp unsalted butter

2 small leeks, white and pale green parts, chopped

2 large eggs

1 cup (240 ml) half-and-half

½ tsp salt

¼ tsp freshly ground pepper

⅛ tsp ground nutmeg

1 cup (125 g) shredded Gruyère cheese

Place the dough on a lightly floured work surface and dust with flour. Roll out the dough into a round about 12 inches (30 cm) in diameter. Transfer the dough to a 9-inch (23-cm) tart pan with a removable bottom, fitting the dough into the bottom and sides of the pan and leaving a ½-inch (12-mm) overhang. Fold the overhanging dough in against the pan sides to form a rim. Line the dough with a piece of aluminum foil and freeze for 30 minutes.

Meanwhile, place a rack in the lower third of the oven and preheat to 375°F (190°C).

Place the tart pan on a baking sheet and fill with pie weights or dried beans. Bake until the dough sets and begins to brown, 15–20 minutes.

Meanwhile, in a frying pan, cook the bacon over medium heat, stirring, until crisp and golden, about 6 minutes. Transfer to paper towels to drain. Discard the fat in the pan and wipe the pan with paper towels. Melt the butter in the pan over medium heat. Add the leeks and cook, stirring occasionally, until tender, about 10 minutes. Transfer to a plate and let cool slightly.

Remove the baking sheet with the tart pan from the oven. Remove the foil and weights. In a bowl, whisk together the eggs, half-and-half, salt, pepper, and nutmeg. Scatter the leeks, bacon, and cheese evenly in the pastry shell and pour in the egg mixture. Bake until the filling is puffed and golden brown, about 30 minutes. Let cool slightly. Remove the sides of the pan, cut the quiche into wedges, and serve warm or at room temperature.

PANCAKES, WAFFLES & FRENCH TOAST

FROM THE GRIDDLE, THE OVEN & THE FRYING PAN

PERFECT PANCAKES

Perfectly lofty, feather-light pancakes are easily achievable if you follow a few basic tips. First, use fresh, quality ingredients; baking soda should be no more than six months old. Next, stir the batter only until the wet and dry ingredients are incorporated; overbeating will make pancakes chewy instead of fluffy. And finally, cook the pancakes on a flat, heavy-bottomed, preheated, and well-greased surface. Each of the following recipes serves four to six.

classic buttermilk pancakes

In a large bowl, stir together the flour, baking powder, baking soda, and salt. In a medium bowl, whisk together the eggs, buttermilk, and melted butter. Add the egg mixture to the flour mixture and stir until incorporated. (The batter will still be slightly lumpy.)

Heat a griddle or a large frying pan over medium heat. Coat generously with melted butter and then ladle about ⅓ cup (80 ml) batter onto the griddle for each pancake. Cook until the edges are golden and bubbles form on the surface, then flip the pancakes and continue cooking until cooked through, about 3 minutes total. Keep warm while you cook the remaining pancakes. Serve hot.

1½ cups (190 g) all-purpose flour

1½ tsp baking powder

¾ tsp baking soda

¼ tsp salt

2 large eggs

2 cups (480 ml) buttermilk

3 tbsp unsalted butter, melted, plus more for cooking

whole-grain buttermilk pancakes

In a large bowl, stir together the whole wheat flour, all-purpose flour, rolled oats, brown sugar, baking powder, baking soda, and salt. In a medium bowl, whisk together the eggs, buttermilk, and melted butter. Add the egg mixture to the flour mixture and stir until incorporated.

Heat a griddle or a large frying pan over medium heat. Coat generously with melted butter and then ladle about ⅓ cup (80 ml) batter onto the griddle for each pancake. Cook until the edges are golden and bubbles form on the surface, then flip the pancakes and continue cooking until cooked through, about 3 minutes total. Keep warm while you cook the remaining pancakes. Serve hot.

1 cup (120 g) whole wheat flour

½ cup (60 g) all-purpose flour

½ cup (45 g) rolled oats

2 tbsp firmly packed dark brown sugar

1½ tsp baking powder

¾ tsp baking soda

¼ tsp salt

2 large eggs

2 cups (480 ml) buttermilk

3 tbsp unsalted butter, melted, plus more for cooking

gluten-free buttermilk pancakes

In a large bowl, stir together the gluten-free flour, sugar, baking powder, and salt. In a medium bowl, whisk together the eggs, buttermilk, milk, and melted butter. Add the egg mixture to the flour mixture and stir until incorporated.

Heat a griddle or a large frying pan over medium-low heat. Coat generously with melted butter and then ladle slightly less than ¼ cup (60 ml) batter onto the griddle for each pancake. Cook without moving until the top looks dry, there are bubbles breaking the entire surface, and the bottom is deeply golden brown, about 4 minutes. Flip the pancakes and continue cooking until deep golden brown and cooked through, about 5 minutes longer. Keep warm while you cook the remaining pancakes. (The batter will thicken as it stands, so add more milk or water as needed, about 1 tbsp at a time, stirring regularly.) Serve the pancakes hot.

2 cups (250 g) gluten-free all-purpose flour

2 tbsp sugar

4 tsp baking powder

½ tsp salt

2 large eggs, at room temperature

2 cups (480 ml) buttermilk, at room temperature

⅓ cup (80 ml) whole milk, at room temperature, plus more as needed

3 tbsp unsalted butter, melted, plus more for cooking

PANCAKE BATTER MIX-INS

½ cup (60 g) sliced strawberries + ½ cup (90 g) chocolate chips

2 tsp pumpkin pie spice + 2 tsp grated orange zest

3 tbsp shredded coconut + ½ cup (90 g) finely chopped drained pineapple

½ cup (60 g) blueberries + 2 tsp grated lemon zest

½ cup (60 g) diced banana

1 tsp poppy seeds + 1 tbsp sesame seeds + 1 tbsp chopped pecans

PANCAKE TOPPINGS

Sweetened whipped cream + fresh blueberries + Blueberry Syrup (page 121)

Diced fresh pineapple + macadamia nuts + shredded coconut + maple syrup

Quick Strawberry Jam (page 120) + sliced toasted almonds

Peanut or almond butter + crumbled bacon + maple syrup

Strawberry syrup + fresh strawberries + whipped cream + shaved chocolate

Mascarpone + fresh or grilled peaches + honey + and powdered sugar

Sugar-and-Spice Butter (page 122) + finely chopped apples + maple syrup

PEANUT BUTTER & BACON
with maple syrup on
buttermilk pancakes

FINISH SWEET
OR SAVORY

Feather-light buttermilk pancakes
are a treat on their own. Add a few
choice toppings and the breakfast
classic becomes truly memorable.

BLUEBERRY SYRUP
with fresh blueberries
on lemon-infused
buttermilk pancakes

PINEAPPLE & COCONUT
with toasted macadamia
nuts and maple syrup
on pineapple-coconut
buttermilk pancakes

PEACHES & MASCARPONE
dusted with confectioners'
sugar on buttermilk pancakes

STRAWBERRIES & CHOCOLATE
with whipped cream and
strawberry syrup on strawberry-
studded buttermilk pancakes

PERFECT WAFFLES

The keys to achieving crispy waffles are a really hot waffle iron (sprinkle with a drop of water and wait for a sizzle) and patience (don't rush the cooking, and no peeking!). Freeze leftovers in a lock-top plastic bag, then rewarm in a toaster. Each recipe serves four to six.

classic waffles

Preheat a waffle maker according to the manufacturer's directions.

In a large bowl, stir together the flour, sugar, baking powder, and salt. In a medium bowl, whisk together the eggs, milk, melted butter, and vanilla. Add the egg mixture to the flour mixture and stir until there are no lumps remaining.

Coat the inside of the waffle maker on both sides with nonstick cooking spray. Ladle about ¾ cup (180 ml) batter onto the waffle maker, close the lid, and cook until the waffles are browned and cooked through, 3–4 minutes.

Using a fork, transfer the waffles to a plate and keep warm while you cook the remaining batter. Serve hot.

1½ cups (190 g) all-purpose flour

3 tbsp sugar

1 tbsp baking powder

¼ tsp salt

2 large eggs

1½ cups (350 ml) whole milk

¼ cup (60 g) unsalted butter, melted and cooled

1 tsp pure vanilla extract

Nonstick cooking spray

whole wheat waffles

Preheat a waffle maker according to the manufacturer's directions.

In a large bowl, stir together the flour, sugar, baking powder, and salt. In a medium bowl, whisk together the eggs, milk, melted butter, and vanilla. Add the egg mixture to the flour mixture and stir until there are no lumps remaining.

Coat the inside of the waffle maker on both sides with nonstick cooking spray. Ladle about ¾ cup (180 ml) batter onto the waffle maker, close the lid, and cook until the waffles are browned and cooked through, 3–4 minutes.

Using a fork, transfer the waffles to a plate and keep warm while you cook the remaining batter. Serve hot.

1½ cups (190 g) whole wheat flour

2 tbsp sugar

2 tsp baking powder

¼ tsp salt

2 large eggs

1½ cups (350 ml) whole milk

⅓ cup (90 g) unsalted butter, melted and cooled

1 tsp pure vanilla extract

Nonstick cooking spray

gluten-free waffles

Preheat a waffle maker according to the manufacturer's directions.

In a large bowl, stir together the gluten-free flour, sugar, baking powder, and salt. In a medium bowl, whisk together the eggs, milk, melted butter, and vanilla. Add the egg mixture to the flour mixture and stir until there are no lumps remaining.

Coat the inside of the waffle maker on both sides with nonstick cooking spray. Ladle about ¾ cup (180 ml) batter onto the waffle maker, close the lid, and cook until the waffles are browned and cooked through, 3–4 minutes. Using a fork, transfer the waffles to a plate and let rest for about 3 minutes to finish cooking on the inside before serving, or keep warm while you cook the remaining batter. Serve hot.

1½ cups (190 g) gluten-free all-purpose flour

3 tbsp sugar

1 tbsp baking powder

¼ tsp salt

2 large eggs

1½ cups (350 ml) plus 1 tbsp whole milk

¼ cup (60 g) unsalted butter, melted and cooled

1 tsp pure vanilla extract

Nonstick cooking spray

WAFFLE BATTER MIX-INS

Grated zest of 1 orange + 1 tbsp fresh orange juice + 1 tbsp fresh thyme leaves

¼ cup (45 g) flaxseeds + 1 mashed banana

1 tbsp chopped macadamia nuts + 1 tbsp dried unsweetened shredded coconut

½ cup (45 g) sweetened cocoa powder + topped with ½ cup (90 g) chopped pitted cherries and Bing Cherry Syrup (page 121)

2 tbsp chopped walnuts + topped with Maple-Pear Sauce (page 121)

WAFFLE TOPPINGS

Mini marshmallows + dark chocolate sauce

Blueberries + yogurt + chia seeds

Mascarpone cheese + grated lemon zest

Peanut butter + banana slices + bacon with maple syrup drizzle

Apple slices + melted Cheddar cheese

Lemon Curd (page 120) + fresh berries + confectioners' sugar

Diced fresh peaches + maple syrup + cinnamon sugar–spiced whipped cream + orange zest

Sliced bananas + toasted pecans + caramel sauce

**PROSCIUTTO + PEARS
+ MAPLE SYRUP**

**COCOA WAFFLE + WHIPPED
CREAM + BING CHERRY SYRUP**

**FRESH BERRIES + LEMON
CURD + EDIBLE BLOSSOMS**

**TOASTED MARSHMALLOWS
+ NUTELLA + HAZELNUTS**

SAUTÉED APPLES + PUMPKIN
PIE–SPICED CREAM + MAPLE SYRUP

PLAY WITH TOPPINGS

With their boxy pockets and crisp exterior, waffles are the perfect receptacles for capturing syrups, sauces, and chunky toppings. In addition to the requisite fruit and nuts, try pairing waffles with proteins for inspired sweet-savory flavors.

SLICED BANANAS + CARAMEL
SAUCE + TOASTED PECANS

FRIED CHICKEN + GRAVY
+ HOT PEPPER SAUCE

For a morning meal served with flourish, few dishes are more dazzling than a perfectly lofty oven pancake.

PEACH & ALMOND DUTCH BABY

SERVES 2–4

The oven pancake known as a Dutch baby looks impressive as it puffs up high when baked. The buttery popover-like shell is the perfect canvas for a variety of ingredients. Peaches are a natural, as are apples, but try any of your favorites.

FOR THE BATTER
⅔ cup (160 ml) whole milk
⅔ cup (80 g) all-purpose flour
¼ tsp salt
3 large eggs
2 tbsp unsalted butter, melted

FOR THE PEACH FILLING
2 tbsp unsalted butter

3 ripe peaches or nectarines, halved, pitted, and sliced
2 tbsp firmly packed light brown sugar
2 tsp fresh lemon juice
¼ cup (30 g) sliced almonds, lightly toasted
Confectioners' sugar for dusting
Whipped cream for serving (optional)

Place a 12-inch (30-cm) ovenproof frying pan in the oven and preheat the oven to 425°F (220°C).

To make the batter, in a blender, combine the milk, flour, salt, and eggs and blend until smooth. With the motor running, drizzle in 1 tbsp of the melted butter and blend until incorporated. Place the remaining 1 tbsp butter in the hot frying pan. Using a pastry brush, brush the butter all over the pan bottom and sides and pour in the batter. Immediately transfer the pan to the oven and bake until puffed and golden, 15–20 minutes.

Meanwhile, make the peach filling: In another large frying pan, melt the butter over medium heat. Add the peaches, brown sugar, and lemon juice and cook, stirring occasionally, until the peaches release their juices and the brown sugar dissolves, about 3 minutes. Remove from the heat.

Remove the pan from the oven. Pour the peaches onto the pancake. Sprinkle with the almonds and dust lightly with confectioners' sugar. Cut into wedges and serve with whipped cream, if desired.

VARIATION

Brown Butter & Caramelized Apple Dutch Baby
Prepare the batter as directed, adding ½ tsp ground cinnamon with the flour; set aside. To make the filling, peel and core 2 Fuji or other baking apples and cut each into 16 wedges. In a 12-inch (30-cm) ovenproof frying pan, melt 3 tbsp unsalted butter over medium-high heat. When the butter begins to brown, add the apples and cook, turning as needed, until golden on all sides, about 5 minutes. Add an additional 1 tbsp butter and heat until melted and bubbling. Pour the batter over the apples in the hot pan. Immediately transfer the pan to the oven and bake as directed. Dust with confectioners' sugar. Serve with maple syrup.

PERFECT CREPES

Whether you're serving savory or sweet crepes, the process for making the batter is the same. Mix the ingredients completely, leaving no lumps (a blender works best), then let the batter rest for at least an hour. Pour just enough batter into the pan to barely cover the bottom and you'll enjoy thin, light crepes. Each recipe makes about 16 crepes.

classic french crepes

In a blender, combine the milk, flour, salt, and eggs and blend until smooth. With the motor running, drizzle in the melted butter and blend until incorporated. Transfer to a bowl, cover, and refrigerate for at least 1 hour or up to 24 hours.

Heat a 6-inch (15-cm) crepe pan or a nonstick frying pan over medium-high heat. Add ½ tsp butter and swirl the pan until the butter melts and covers the bottom of the pan. (If you are using a nonstick pan, you will need to butter the pan again before cooking each crepe.) Ladle about ¼ cup (60 ml) batter into the pan and tilt the pan to cover the bottom evenly. Cook until the crepe is lightly browned underneath, 1–2 minutes. Carefully run a spatula around the edges of the pan to loosen the crepe (do not cook the other side) and transfer to a plate. Serve the crepes one at a time, or repeat to cook the remaining batter, stacking the crepes on the plate until all are cooked. Fill and top the crepes as desired and serve.

2 cups (480 ml) whole milk

2 cups (250 g) all-purpose flour

1 tsp salt

4 large eggs

4 tbsp (60 g) unsalted butter, melted and cooled, plus butter for cooking

gluten-free crepes

In a blender, combine the milk, eggs, and 2 tbsp water and pulse a few times to mix. Add the gluten-free flour and salt and blend until smooth. With the motor running, drizzle in the melted butter and blend until incorporated. Transfer to a bowl, cover, and refrigerate for at least 1 hour or up to 24 hours. The batter should be thin and very pourable; if needed, stir in 1–2 tbsp more water. Cook the crepes as directed above.

2 cups (480 ml) whole milk

4 large eggs

2 cups (250 g) gluten-free all-purpose flour

1 tsp salt

4 tbsp (60 g) unsalted butter, melted and cooled, plus butter for cooking

buckwheat crepes

In a blender, combine the milk, both flours, salt, and eggs and blend until smooth. With the motor running, drizzle in the melted butter and blend until incorporated. Transfer to a bowl, cover, and refrigerate for at least 1 hour or up to 24 hours.

Heat a 6-inch (15-cm) crepe pan or a nonstick frying pan over medium-high heat. Add ½ tsp butter and swirl the pan until the butter melts and covers the bottom of the pan. (If you are using a nonstick pan, you will need to butter the pan again before cooking each crepe.) Ladle about ¼ cup (60 ml) batter into the pan and tilt the pan to cover the bottom evenly. Cook until the crepe is lightly browned underneath, 1–2 minutes. Carefully run a spatula around the edges of the pan to loosen the crepe (do not cook the other side) and transfer to a plate. Serve the crepes one at a time, or repeat to cook the remaining batter, stacking the crepes on the plate until all are cooked. Fill and top the crepes as desired and serve.

1½ cups (350 ml) whole milk

1 cup (120 g) buckwheat flour

½ cup (60 g) all-purpose flour

¾ tsp salt

4 large eggs

4 tbsp (60 g) unsalted butter, melted and cooled, plus butter for cooking

CREPE BATTER MIX-INS

2 tbsp finely chopped fresh herbs

1 tbsp orange liqueur such as Cointreau

2 tbsp finely chopped drained sun-dried tomatoes

2 tbsp grated citrus zest

CREPE FILLINGS (PER CREPE)

2 tbsp Nutella + ½ sliced banana

2 tbsp Lemon Curd (page 120) + ½ cup (60 g) raspberries

2 slices ham + 1 oz (30 g) shredded Gruyère cheese + ½ sliced plum tomato

2 slices smoked turkey + 1 oz (30 g) shredded Cheddar cheese + ¼ cup (45 g) thinly sliced pears

1 oz (30 g) Brie cheese + ¼ cup (45 g) thinly sliced nectarines

CREPE TOPPINGS

Whipped cream + berries

Caramel sauce + chopped pecans

Lemon juice + confectioners' sugar

Ricotta cheese + honey + cinnamon

Hot fudge + pomegranate seeds

CLASSIC FRENCH TOAST

SERVES 4

To make good French toast, use day-old bread because the drier the bread is, the more it will absorb the egg mixture. Use bread slices about ¾ inch (2 cm) thick for the best results and add vanilla extract to the egg mixture for greater depth of flavor.

6 large eggs

1½ cups (350 ml) whole milk or half-and-half

1 tbsp pure vanilla extract

½ tsp ground cinnamon

Pinch of ground nutmeg

8 slices day-old brioche, challah, or French bread, sliced about ¾ inch (2 cm) thick

2 tbsp unsalted butter

Confectioners' sugar for dusting

Strawberry-Rhubarb Compote (page 120) or pure maple syrup, warmed, for serving

Sweetened whipped cream for serving

In a large bowl, whisk together the eggs, milk, vanilla, cinnamon, and nutmeg.

Place the bread slices in a single layer in a large, shallow baking dish and pour the egg mixture over the top. Soak the bread for 10 minutes, flipping halfway through.

In a large frying pan, melt 1 tbsp of the butter over medium heat. Place half the bread slices in the pan and cook, turning once, until golden brown, about 3 minutes per side. Transfer to a serving plate and keep warm. Melt the remaining 1 tbsp butter in the pan and cook the remaining bread slices. Dust the French toast with confectioners' sugar and serve with the warm compote and whipped cream.

VARIATION

Nut-Crusted French Toast with Blueberries
Make the egg mixture and soak the bread slices as directed. Spread 1½ cups (185 g) chopped pecans, walnuts, or hazelnuts on a plate. Remove half the bread slices, one at a time, from the egg mixture and lightly press each slice into the nuts, coating only one side.

Place the bread, nut side down, in the buttered pan and cook as directed. Transfer to a serving plate and keep warm. Melt the remaining butter in the pan, then coat and cook the remaining bread slices. Serve with 2 cups (280 g) blueberries and warm maple syrup.

A chunky compote of strawberries and rhubarb adds bright flavor. Balance its sweet-tartness with a generous dollop of whipped cream.

BAKED FRENCH TOAST WITH PEARS & CARDAMOM

SERVES 6

This cross between bread pudding and French toast is an ideal make-ahead brunch dish. Blend the egg mixture and add the bread cubes to soak the evening before you plan to serve it. Bake in the morning, then serve hot from the oven with plenty of maple syrup and a sifter of confectioners' sugar for serving.

3 tbsp unsalted butter

2 pears, such as Bosc, Bartlett, or Anjou, peeled, cored, and cut into 1-inch (2.5-cm) pieces

2 tbsp firmly packed dark brown sugar

½ tsp ground cardamom

½ loaf (½ lb/250 g) challah, cut into 1-inch (2.5-cm) cubes

4 large eggs

1 cup (240 ml) whole milk

1 tsp pure vanilla extract

Use 1 tbsp of the butter to coat the bottom and sides of a 9-by-13-inch (23-by-33-cm) baking dish that is 2 inches (5 cm) deep.

In a large frying pan, melt the remaining 2 tbsp butter over medium-high heat. Add the pears, brown sugar, and cardamom and cook, stirring occasionally, until softened, about 5 minutes. Transfer the pears and all of the butter from the pan to a bowl. Add the bread cubes to the bowl and toss until well combined. Transfer the bread mixture to the prepared baking dish and spread in an even layer.

In the same bowl used for the bread, whisk together the eggs, milk, and vanilla and pour over the bread. Let stand at room temperature for 1 hour, or cover and refrigerate for up to 24 hours.

Preheat the oven to 350°F (180°C). Uncover the baking dish and bake until golden brown, about 40 minutes. Let cool slightly, then spoon onto individual plates. Serve hot.

FRENCH TOAST STUFFED WITH CREAM CHEESE & STRAWBERRY JAM

SERVES 6

Vary this elegant take on French toast with any of your favorite filling ingredients. Try apricot preserves and mascarpone, peanut butter and raspberry jam, or Nutella. Challah is a good choice for this dish because pockets can be easily cut into thick slices; a solid brioche loaf or pain de mie would also work well.

6 oz (180 g) cream cheese, at room temperature

⅓ cup (105 g) strawberry jam

1 loaf (1 lb/500 g) challah

5 large eggs

1¼ cups (300 ml) whole milk

1 tsp pure vanilla extract

2 tbsp unsalted butter

Pure maple syrup, warmed, for serving

In a small bowl, stir together the cream cheese and jam.

Cut the challah into 6 slices, each about 2½ inches (6 cm) thick. Using a small, sharp knife, cut through the crust on one side of each bread slice to make a pocket, leaving a 1-inch (2.5-cm) border uncut. Using a small spoon, stuff the pockets with the cream cheese mixture.

In a large bowl, whisk together the eggs, milk, and vanilla. In a large frying pan, melt 1 tbsp of the butter over medium heat. Dip 3 of the stuffed bread slices into the egg mixture, coating both sides and letting the excess drip back into the bowl. Place the bread in the pan and cook, turning once, until golden brown, about 4 minutes per side. Transfer to a serving plate and keep warm. Melt the remaining 1 tbsp butter in the pan and cook the remaining 3 stuffed bread slices. Serve with warm maple syrup.

BREADS & PASTRIES

DOUGHNUTS, BUNS, MUFFINS, SCONES, TARTS & COFFEE CAKES

CINNAMON ROLLS WITH CREAM CHEESE ICING

MAKES 8 ROLLS

This recipe makes irresistible, fist-size cinnamon rolls. Make the dough and shape the rolls the night before you plan to serve them so you can sleep in.

FOR THE DOUGH

1 cup (240 ml) whole milk

½ cup (100 g) granulated sugar

5 tbsp (75 g) unsalted butter, melted and cooled, plus butter for greasing

3 large eggs

1 package (2¼ tsp) quick-rise yeast

5 cups (620 g) all-purpose flour, plus more for dusting

1¼ tsp salt

FOR THE FILLING

½ cup (100 g) firmly packed light brown sugar

6 tbsp (90 g) unsalted butter, at room temperature

2 tsp ground cinnamon

Cream Cheese Icing (page 121)

To make the dough, in the bowl of a stand mixer fitted with the paddle attachment, combine the milk, granulated sugar, melted butter, eggs, and yeast. Add 4½ cups (550 g) of the flour and the salt. Beat on medium-low speed, adding a little more flour if needed to make a soft dough that does not stick to the bowl. Switch to the dough hook and knead the dough on medium-low speed, adding more flour if needed, until the dough is smooth but still soft, 6–7 minutes. Shape the dough into a ball. Butter a large bowl. Add the dough, turn to coat with the butter, and cover tightly with plastic wrap. Let the dough rise in a warm spot until doubled in size, 1½–2 hours.

To make the filling, in the clean bowl of the stand mixer fitted with the clean paddle attachment, beat the brown sugar, butter, and cinnamon on medium speed until combined, about 30 seconds.

Punch down the dough and turn out onto a floured work surface. Dust the top with flour. Roll out into a rectangle about 14 by 16 inches (35 by 40 cm), with a long side facing you. Spread the filling evenly over the dough, leaving a 1-inch (2.5-cm) border at the top and bottom. Starting at the long side farthest from you, roll up the rectangle into a log. Pinch the seams to seal. Cut the log crosswise into 8 equal slices.

Butter a 9-by-13-inch (23-by-33-cm) baking pan or a large, heavy ovenproof frying pan. Arrange the slices, cut side up, in the pan. Cover loosely with plastic wrap and let rise in a warm spot until doubled in size, 1¼–1½ hours. (Alternatively, refrigerate overnight until doubled, 8–12 hours, then let stand at room temperature for 1 hour before baking.)

Preheat the oven to 350°F (180°C). Bake until the rolls are golden brown, about 30 minutes. Let cool in the pan on a wire rack for 15 minutes. Meanwhile, make the icing. Drizzle the icing over the warm rolls, or pour the icing over the rolls and spread evenly with a metal icing spatula. Let cool for 15 minutes. Serve the rolls warm or at room temperature.

For an easy variation, sprinkle ½ cup (90 g) raisins or chopped toasted pecans over the cinnamon butter before rolling up the dough.

RASPBERRY-LEMON MUFFINS

MAKES 12 MUFFINS

A freshly-baked muffin is always a welcome treat in the morning. This raspberry-studded version rises nicely in the oven and reveals a light, cakey interior underneath a crisp, sugar-coated top crust. To change it up, add fresh blueberries and a crisp almond streusel topping (below).

2 cups (250 g) all-purpose flour

⅔ cup (155 g) firmly packed light brown sugar

½ tsp baking powder

½ tsp baking soda

½ tsp ground cinnamon

¼ tsp salt

1 cup (125 g) fresh or frozen raspberries

1 cup (240 ml) buttermilk

2 large eggs

5 tbsp (75 g) unsalted butter, melted and cooled, plus more for greasing (optional)

2 tsp grated lemon zest

½ tsp pure vanilla extract

1 tbsp turbinado sugar

Preheat the oven to 400°F (200°C). Line 12 standard muffin cups with paper liners or butter the cups.

In a large bowl, stir together the flour, brown sugar, baking powder, baking soda, cinnamon, and salt. Gently fold in the raspberries. In a medium bowl, whisk together the buttermilk, eggs, and melted butter. Add the lemon zest and vanilla and whisk just until blended. Pour the buttermilk mixture over the flour mixture and stir just until combined. Divide the batter evenly among the prepared muffin cups. Sprinkle the turbinado sugar evenly over the muffin tops.

Bake until the muffins are golden brown and a toothpick inserted into the center of a muffin comes out almost clean, about 20 minutes if using fresh raspberries or 25 minutes if using frozen. Let cool in the pan on a wire rack for 15 minutes, then unmold the muffins onto the rack and let cool a bit more before serving.

VARIATION

Blueberry Muffins with Almond Streusel
Omit the cinnamon and lemon zest, and substitute 1½ cups (185 g) fresh or frozen blueberries for the raspberries. For the topping, replace the turbinado sugar with almond streusel: In a small bowl, mix ¼ cup (45 g) all-purpose flour, 2 tbsp granulated sugar, and 2 tbsp room-temperature unsalted butter with your fingertips until combined, then work in ⅓ cup (45 g) sliced almonds. Sprinkle the streusel over the muffin tops and bake as directed.

ENGLISH CREAM SCONES

MAKES 8 SCONES

These buttery scones have a delicate texture and mildly sweet flavor that begs for a generous spoonful of fresh fruit jam (page 120). For a departure from the traditional preparation, opt for savory cheddar and bacon scones or sweet candied ginger scones (below).

2 cups (250 g) all-purpose flour, plus more for dusting

3 tbsp sugar

2½ tsp baking powder

¼ tsp salt

½ cup (125 g) cold unsalted butter, cut into cubes

½ cup (90 g) dried currants

1 cup (240 ml) heavy cream

Preheat the oven to 400°F (200°C). Line a baking sheet with parchment paper.

In a bowl, stir together the flour, sugar, baking powder, and salt. Using a pastry blender or 2 knives, cut the butter into the flour mixture just until the mixture forms coarse crumbs about the size of peas. Stir in the currants. Pour the cream over the flour mixture and stir with a fork or a rubber spatula just until combined.

Turn the dough out onto a lightly floured work surface. Using floured hands, pat out into a round about ½ inch (12 mm) thick. Using a 3-inch (7.5-cm) biscuit cutter, cut out as many rounds of the dough as possible. Gather up the scraps and knead briefly, then pat out the dough and cut out more rounds to make a total of 8 scones. Place 1 inch (2.5 cm) apart on the prepared baking sheet.

Bake until the scones are golden brown, 17–20 minutes. Let cool slightly on the baking sheet. Serve warm or at room temperature.

VARIATIONS

Bacon, Cheddar & Green Onion Scones
Stir together the flour mixture as directed, reducing the sugar to 2 tsp. Omit the currants and substitute 1 cup (115 g) diced Cheddar cheese, 1 cup (60 g) crumbled fried bacon, and ⅓ cup (30 g) finely sliced green onions (green part only) or chives. Stir in the cream, shape, and bake as directed.

Ginger Scones
Omit the currants and substitute ½ cup (90 g) chopped crystallized ginger. Brush the unbaked scones with a beaten egg white, sprinkle with 1 tbsp turbinado sugar, and bake as directed.

CLASSIC POPOVERS

MAKES 12 POPOVERS

The best popovers boast a dramatic rise in the oven, a lovely browned and crisp crust, and moist, hollow interiors that provide the perfect medium for warm butter and your favorite jam. A popover pan (shown left) is designed with deep and separate cups to promote an even distribution of heat and will ensure the best puff, but a standard muffin pan will also work well.

1 cup (120 g) all-purpose flour

½ tsp salt

1 cup (240 ml) whole milk

2 large eggs, at room temperature, beaten

4 tbsp (60 g) unsalted butter, melted, plus room-temperature butter for serving (optional)

Jam of your choice for serving

Preheat the oven to 450°F (230°C).

In a bowl, stir together the flour and salt. Make a well in the center of the flour mixture, add the milk and eggs, and whisk just until combined. Pour the batter into a glass measuring cup or a pitcher.

Place a 12-cup popover pan or standard muffin pan in the oven and heat until hot, about 2 minutes. Remove from the oven and spoon 1 tsp of the melted butter into each cup. Divide the batter evenly among the cups, filling them half-full.

Bake for 10 minutes. Reduce the oven temperature to 375°F (190°C) and continue to bake, without opening the oven door, until the popovers are puffed, crisp, and golden brown, 20–25 minutes longer. Using your fingers, gently remove the piping-hot popovers from the pan and serve right away with butter, if desired, and jam.

PECAN STICKY BUNS

MAKES 16 BUNS

It's hard to resist the decadent appeal of sticky buns. Streamline your morning routine by making them ahead. Let rise in the refrigerator overnight for baking the next day.

FOR THE DOUGH

1 package (2¼ tsp) active dry yeast

¾ cup (180 ml) whole milk, warmed (110°F/43°C)

¼ cup (60 g) granulated sugar

4 large eggs

4½ cups (550 g) all-purpose flour, plus more as needed

1½ tsp salt

6 tbsp (90 g) unsalted butter, cut into chunks, plus more for greasing

FOR THE CARAMEL

6 tbsp (90 g) unsalted butter, melted

1 cup (200 g) firmly packed light brown sugar

3 tbsp dark honey

Pinch of salt

1 cup (125 g) coarsely chopped pecans

4 tbsp (60 g) unsalted butter, at room temperature

½ cup (100 g) firmly packed light brown sugar

1 tsp ground cinnamon

To make the dough, in the bowl of a stand mixer, dissolve the yeast in the warm milk and let stand until foamy, about 10 minutes. Add the granulated sugar, eggs, flour, and salt. Attach the dough hook and knead on low speed, adding a little more flour if needed, until the ingredients come together. Toss in the butter and continue to knead until the dough is smooth and springy, about 7 minutes. Lightly butter a large bowl. Form the dough into a ball, place in the bowl, and cover with plastic wrap. Let the dough rise at room temperature until doubled in size, 1½–2 hours.

Butter two 9-inch (23-cm) round cake pans. Make the caramel: In a bowl, stir together the melted butter, brown sugar, honey, salt, and pecans. Spread half of the caramel mixture in each pan.

Punch down the dough, turn out onto a floured work surface, and cut it in half. Roll out each half into a rectangle about 8 by 14 inches (20 by 35 cm). Spread each rectangle with 2 tbsp of the room-temperature butter, then half each of the brown sugar and cinnamon, leaving ½ inch (12 mm) of a long side uncovered. Starting at a side opposite the uncovered one, roll up each rectangle into a log and pinch the seam to seal. Cut each log crosswise into 8 equal slices. Arrange the slices, cut side up, in the pans. Cover loosely with plastic wrap and let rise in a warm spot until puffy, about 1 hour. (Or, refrigerate overnight and let stand at room temperature for 1 hour before baking.)

Preheat the oven to 350°F (180°C). Bake until the buns are golden brown, 30–35 minutes. Let cool in the pans on a wire rack for 5 minutes, then carefully invert each pan onto a plate and unmold the buns. When they are still warm but cool enough not to burn your fingers, pull them apart and dig in.

RAISED DOUGHNUTS

MAKES 8–10 DOUGHNUTS AND HOLES

Few morning treats start the day off with more promise than a perfectly glazed and decorated doughnut. Don't be intimidated by the frying step; it's easier than you think.

1 cup (250 ml) whole milk, warmed (110°F/43°C)

1 package (2¼ tsp) instant yeast

3 tbsp vegetable shortening, melted and cooled slightly

1 large egg

¼ cup (60 g) sugar

2 tsp salt

3 cups (370 g) all-purpose flour, plus more for dusting

Canola oil for greasing and frying

Glaze or sugar coating of choice (recipes on pages 122–123; ideas on pages 98–99)

Sprinkles or other toppings (optional)

Pour the warm milk into a small bowl, sprinkle the yeast on top, and stir gently. Let stand in a warm spot until foamy, 5–10 minutes.

Transfer the yeast mixture to the bowl of a stand mixer fitted with the paddle attachment. Add the shortening, egg, sugar, salt, and 1½ cups (190 g) of the flour and beat on low speed until combined, about 2 minutes. Add the remaining 1½ cups (190 g) flour, raise the speed to medium, and beat until incorporated, about 30 seconds. Switch to the dough hook and knead on medium speed until the dough is smooth and pulls away from the bowl, 3–4 minutes. Oil a large bowl. Transfer the dough to the bowl and cover with a kitchen towel. Let the dough rise in a warm spot until doubled in size, about 1 hour.

Punch down the dough, turn out onto a floured work surface, and roll out ½ inch (12 mm) thick. Using a doughnut cutter or 2 different-size round cutters (3½ inch/9 cm and 1 inch/2.5 cm), cut out doughnuts and holes. Transfer to a floured baking sheet, cover with a kitchen towel, and let rise in a warm spot until doubled in size, about 1 hour.

Meanwhile, make the glaze or prepare the sugar coating of your choice. Set aside.

Pour canola oil to a depth of 2 inches (5 cm) into a deep-fryer or deep, heavy sauté pan and warm over medium-high heat until it registers 360°F (182°C) on a deep-frying thermometer. Line a baking sheet with paper towels. Carefully lower 2–5 doughnuts or holes into the hot oil and deep-fry until dark golden, about 1½ minutes. Turn over and cook until dark golden on the second side, about 1 minute longer. Transfer to the prepared baking sheet. Fry the remaining doughnuts and holes, allowing the oil to return to 360°F (182°C) between batches.

When the doughnuts and holes are cool enough to handle but are still warm, dip the tops in the glaze or coating, letting any excess fall back into the bowl. Decorate with sprinkles or other toppings, if desired. Place on a wire rack until the glaze sets, about 30 minutes, and serve.

MAPLE GLAZE
+ BACON

STRAWBERRY GLAZE
+ CONFETTI SPRINKLES

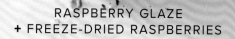

RASPBERRY GLAZE
+ FREEZE-DRIED RASPBERRIES

LAVENDER GLAZE
+ CANDIED VIOLETS

CINNAMON
+ SUGAR

LEMON GLAZE
+ ZEST

CHOCOLATE GLAZE
+ TOASTED SHAVED COCONUT

ROSE-TINTED VANILLA GLAZE
+ FRESH EDIBLE BLOSSOMS

FRESH FRUIT TARTS

Using frozen puff pastry, it's quick and easy to make sweet tarts, and the combinations are endless. Cut a sheet of purchased puff pastry into four single-serving pastry squares, brush with egg, and par-bake. Layer the pastry shells with fruit, brush with glaze, and continue baking to golden perfection.

easy fruit tarts

Preheat the oven to 400°F (200°C). Line a baking sheet with parchment paper.

On a lightly floured work surface, gently roll out the puff pastry into a 9-inch (23-cm) square. Using a sharp paring knife, cut the pastry into 4 equal squares, then gently score a ¾-inch (2-cm) border around each square, carefully cutting halfway through the pastry. Using a fork, prick the center of each square to prevent puffing while baking.

Place the pastry squares well apart on the prepared baking sheet. Brush the entire surface of each square with the egg mixture and bake for 7 minutes. Remove the pan from the oven and add the topping(s) and glaze of your choice to the pastry shells as directed below. Return the pan to the oven and bake until the pastries are golden brown and the fruit is tender, about 10 minutes longer.

All-purpose flour for dusting

1 sheet frozen puff pastry, thawed but still very cold

1 large egg beaten with 1 tsp water

blood oranges & marmalade

Spread 1 tbsp marmalade over the bottom of each pastry shell. Arrange the orange segments, slightly overlapping, over the marmalade. In a small bowl, mix the remaining 2 tbsp marmalade with 1 tsp warm water and brush over the oranges. Finish baking as directed.

6 tbsp (110 g) orange marmalade

2 blood oranges, peeled and cut into segments

apple & cinnamon sugar

Spread 1 tbsp jelly over the bottom of each pastry shell. Arrange 2 or 3 apple slices over the jelly on each tart. In a small bowl, mix the remaining 2 tbsp jelly with 1 tsp warm water and brush over the apples. Sprinkle with cinnamon sugar and finish baking as directed.

6 tbsp apple jelly

1 Granny Smith or other baking apple, cut crosswise into very thin slices

Cinnamon sugar

raspberries & nutella

Spread 1 tbsp Nutella over the bottom of each pastry shell. Arrange the raspberries in a single layer over the Nutella. Brush the jam mixture evenly over the raspberries. Finish baking as directed.

4 tbsp (60 g) Nutella

½ pint (125 g) raspberries

2 tbsp raspberry jam mixed with 1 tsp warm water

rhubarb & strawberry jam

Spread 1 tbsp jam over the bottom of each pastry shell. Arrange sliced rhubarb in a single layer on top. In a small bowl, mix the remaining 2 tbsp jam with 1 tsp warm water and brush over the rhubarb. Finish baking as directed.

6 tbsp (110 g) strawberry jam

1 stalk rhubarb, trimmed, cut crosswise into 3-inch (8 cm) pieces, then cut lengthwise into thin slices

blackberries & lemon curd

Spread 1 tbsp lemon curd over the bottom of each pastry shell. Arrange the blackberries in a single layer over the curd. Brush the jam mixture evenly over the blackberries. Finish baking as directed. Sprinkle with basil leaves, if using, just before serving.

4 tbsp (60 ml) Lemon Curd (page 120)

1 pint (250 g) blackberries

2 tbsp blackberry jam mixed with 1 tsp warm water

Fresh basil leaves for garnish (optional)

apricots & pistachios

Spread 1 tbsp jam over the bottom of each pastry shell. Arrange the apricot wedges, slightly overlapping, on top. In a small bowl, mix the remaining 2 tbsp jam with 1 tsp warm water and brush over the apricots. Sprinkle the chopped pistachios evenly over each pastry. Finish baking as directed.

6 tbsp apricot jam

6–8 fresh apricots, pitted, and cut into thin wedges

¼ cup (30 g) chopped raw pistachios

fresh currants & jelly

Spread 2 tbsp jelly over the bottom of each pastry shell. Finish baking as directed. Top each tart with fresh currants, then dust with confectioners' sugar.

8 tbsp currant jelly

4–8 fresh currant sprigs

Confectioners' sugar

pears & toasted almonds

Spread 1 heaping tbsp jam-cheese mixture over the bottom of each pastry shell. Arrange the sliced pears, slightly overlapping, over the top. Brush the jam mixture evenly over the pear. Finish baking as directed. Sprinkle with almonds just before serving.

2 tbsp pear jam mixed with 3 tbsp cream cheese, at room temperature

1–2 pears, peeled, cored, and sliced

2 tbsp pear jam mixed with 1 tsp warm water

2 tbsp chopped toasted almonds

RHUBARB
+ STRAWBERRY JAM

BLACKBERRIES + BASIL
+ LEMON CURD

APPLE + CINNAMON SUGAR
+ APPLE JELLY

FRESH CURRANTS
+ CURRANT JELLY

PEAR + ALMONDS
+ PEAR GLAZE

RASPBERRIES + NUTELLA
+ RASPBERRY GLAZE

BLOOD ORANGE
+ ORANGE MARMALADE

APRICOT + PISTACHIOS
+ APRICOT GLAZE

BANANA BREAD

MAKES ONE LOAF; SERVES 8–10

Dense and sweet with a tender crumb and deep banana flavor, this recipe for a generously proportioned quick bread is one you'll turn to again and again. Use really ripe, evenly brown-speckled bananas for the best taste and moist texture.

2¼ cups (280 g) all-purpose flour, plus more for dusting

1 cup (250 g) sugar

1 tsp baking soda

½ tsp salt

3 very ripe bananas

½ cup (125 g) unsalted butter, melted, plus more for greasing

2 large eggs, lightly beaten

⅓ cup (90 g) plain yogurt

1 tsp pure vanilla extract

1 cup (125 g) chopped walnuts (optional)

Preheat the oven to 350°F (180°C). Butter a 9-by-5-inch (23-by-13-cm) loaf pan, then dust with flour, tapping out the excess.

In a bowl, stir together the flour, sugar, baking soda, and salt. In a large bowl, mash the bananas well with a fork; you should have about 1½ cups (340 g). Add the melted butter, eggs, yogurt, and vanilla and stir until blended. Gradually add the flour mixture to the banana mixture, stirring gently just until combined. Stir in half of the walnuts, if using. Scrape the batter into the prepared pan. Sprinkle the top with the remaining walnuts, if using.

Bake until a toothpick inserted into the center of the bread comes out clean, about 1 hour. If the top begins to brown too much during baking, cover loosely with aluminum foil. Let cool in the pan on a wire rack for 10 minutes, then turn the loaf out onto the rack, turn right side up, and let cool completely. Cut into slices and serve.

ZUCCHINI BREAD

PUMPKIN BREAD

BANANA BREAD

ZUCCHINI BREAD

MAKES ONE LOAF; SERVES 8–10

With its abundant moisture and mild squash-like flavor, zucchini works well as an ingredient in quick bread. Don't drain any accumulated liquid from the grated zucchini, as it adds moistness to the bread. Add a handful of walnuts to the batter just before scraping it into the pan, if you wish.

½ lb (250 g) zucchini, trimmed	1½ cups (190 g) all-purpose flour, plus more for dusting
¾ cup (185 g) sugar	2 tsp baking powder
½ cup (125 ml) canola oil	1½ tsp ground cinnamon
2 large eggs	½ tsp salt
1 tsp pure vanilla extract	¼ tsp baking soda

Preheat the oven to 350°F (180°C). Grease and lightly flour three 6-by-3-inch (15-by-7.5-cm) loaf pans or one 9-by-5-inch (23-by-13-cm) loaf pan.

Using the large holes on a box grater, shred the zucchini. You should have about 1 cup (150 g). Set aside.

In a large bowl, combine the sugar, canola oil, eggs, and vanilla. Beat vigorously with a whisk or with an electric mixer on medium speed until pale and creamy, about 1 minute. Stir in the zucchini until blended.

In a medium bowl, stir together the flour, baking powder, cinnamon, salt, and baking soda. Add the flour mixture to the zucchini mixture and stir just until combined. The batter will be stiff. Scrape the batter into the prepared pan(s).

Bake until the bread is firm to the touch and pulls away from the pan sides, 35–40 minutes for small loaves or 50–60 minutes for a large loaf. A toothpick inserted into the center of a loaf should come out clean. Let cool in the pan(s) on a wire rack for 10 minutes, then turn the loaves out onto the rack, turn right side up, and let cool completely. Cut into slices and serve.

PUMPKIN BREAD

MAKES TWO LOAVES; SERVES 8–10 EACH

Perfectly moist and flavorful, with a tender, even crumb and ready infusion of spices, this nicely domed pumpkin bread is one you'll appreciate all year long. This recipe makes two ample loaves. Wrap the extra one in plastic wrap and refrigerate for up to 4 days, or add an exterior layer of aluminum foil and freeze for up to 6 months.

Unsalted butter for greasing

3 cups (370 g) all-purpose flour, plus more for dusting

1½ tsp baking soda

1½ tsp salt

1 tsp baking powder

1 tsp *each* ground cinnamon, ground cloves, and ground nutmeg

1 can (15 oz/430 g) pumpkin purée

3 cups (600 g) sugar

1 cup (240 ml) canola oil

3 large eggs, at room temperature

1 tsp pure vanilla extract

½ cup (60 g) pepitas (optional)

Preheat the oven to 350°F (180°C). Butter two 9-by-5-inch (23-by-13-cm) loaf pans, then dust with flour, tapping out the excess.

In a medium bowl, stir together the flour, baking soda, salt, baking powder, cinnamon, cloves, and nutmeg. In a large bowl, stir together the pumpkin purée, sugar, canola oil, eggs, and vanilla until well mixed. Stir in the flour mixture just until combined. Divide the batter evenly between the prepared pans. Sprinkle the pepitas, if using, evenly over the tops.

Bake until the tops are lightly browned and a toothpick inserted into the center of the bread comes out clean, 50–55 minutes. Let cool in the pans on wire racks for 10 minutes, then turn the loaves out onto the racks, turn right side up, and let cool completely. Cut into slices and serve.

PROSCIUTTO + FRESH
MOZZARELLA + BASIL

SLICED TOMATOES
+ SCRAMBLED EGGS + CHIVES

SUN-DRIED TOMATO CREAM CHEESE
+ CARROT + AVOCADO + OLIVES

BLUEBERRIES + CREAM CHEESE
+ HONEY + FRESH EDIBLE BLOSSOMS

SMOKED TROUT + CREAM CHEESE
+ CAPER BERRIES + RED ONION

CHERRY TOMATOES + CAMBOZOLA
+ BACON + ARUGULA

NUTELLA + SLICED BANANAS
+ PISTACHIOS + TOASTED COCONUT

LOAD-YOUR-OWN BAGEL

A bagel bar is a terrific way to entertain a crowd. Just set out all the ingredients and let guests assemble their own perfect combination. When creating a bagel bar, keep a few things in mind. First, bagels are best when purchased the day you'll be serving them. Also, the easiest way to toast multiple bagels is to cut them in half horizontally and place, cut side up, on a baking sheet, then broil until golden brown. Finally, let cream cheese and flavored shmears stand at room temperature for 1 hour before serving for optimal flavor.

APPLESAUCE & BROWN SUGAR CRUMB CAKE

SERVES 12

Serve thick squares of this crumb-topped coffee cake alongside mugs of steaming hot joe. The recipe is an easy one. For a shortcut, mix the streusel the night before; prepare the batter in the morning and top it with the sugary mixture right before baking. For individual cakes, swap out the baking pan for 18 paper-lined muffin cups.

Unsalted butter for greasing

3 cups (370 g) all-purpose flour, plus more for dusting

1 tsp baking soda

1 tsp ground cinnamon

¼ tsp salt

1 cup (200 g) granulated sugar

1 cup (200 g) firmly packed light brown sugar

¾ cup (180 ml) canola oil

¾ cup (220 g) unsweetened applesauce

3 large eggs

3 Golden Delicious or Empire apples, peeled, cored, and cut into cubes

FOR THE STREUSEL

1 cup (120 g) all-purpose flour

½ cup (120 g) cold unsalted butter, cut into chunks

½ cup (100 g) firmly packed light brown sugar

Preheat the oven to 350°F (180°C). Lightly butter a 9-by-13-inch (23-by-33-cm) baking pan, then dust with flour, tapping out the excess.

In a large bowl, stir together the flour, baking soda, cinnamon, and salt. In a medium bowl, whisk together both sugars, canola oil, applesauce, and eggs. Make a well in the center of the flour mixture, add the sugar mixture, and stir just until smooth. Add the apples and stir until combined. Spread the batter in the prepared pan, smoothing the top.

To make the streusel, in a bowl, combine the flour, butter, and brown sugar. Using your fingers, work the ingredients together just until combined. Press the mixture together into a ball and then separate with your fingers into coarse crumbs. Sprinkle the streusel evenly over the top of the cake.

Bake until a toothpick inserted into the center of the cake comes out clean, about 1 hour. Let cool completely in the pan on a wire rack. Cut into squares and serve.

ORANGE MARMALADE BREAD PUDDING

SERVES 8

Simple, fast, and delicious—there's good reason why old-fashioned bread-and-butter pudding is an enduring favorite. Use dry, day-old bread if you can; it soaks up the custard like a sponge yet keeps its shape while baking. This recipe is an easy one to vary. It is superb prepared plain (as here), or baked with apples (below).

3 tbsp unsalted butter, at room temperature, plus more for greasing

1 loaf (1 lb/500 g) day-old challah or brioche, ends trimmed, cut into 12 slices

3 large eggs plus 5 large egg yolks

1¾ cups (420 ml) whole milk

1 cup (240 ml) heavy cream

⅓ cup (90 g) sugar

1 tsp pure vanilla extract

½ tsp salt

Pinch of ground cinnamon

Pinch of ground nutmeg

½ cup (155 g) orange marmalade

Whipped cream for serving

Preheat the oven to 325°F (165°C). Generously butter a 12-inch (30-cm) round or 9-by-13-inch (23-by-33-cm) baking dish.

Spread the challah slices thickly and evenly with the butter. Cut the slices in half crosswise. Lay the slices in the dish so that they overlap slightly.

In a bowl, whisk together the eggs, egg yolks, milk, cream, sugar, vanilla, salt, cinnamon, and nutmeg. Pour evenly over the bread. Let stand at room temperature for about 30 minutes so that the bread soaks up the egg mixture, occasionally pressing down on the slices with a spatula.

Bake the pudding for 30 minutes. Meanwhile, in a small saucepan, gently warm the marmalade over medium-low heat, stirring often. Remove the pudding from the oven and carefully spread the marmalade over the top. Continue to bake until the top is crisp, brown, and sticky, about 10 minutes longer. Let stand for about 10 minutes, then garnish with whipped cream and serve.

VARIATION

Apple & Cinnamon-Raisin Bread Pudding
Preheat the oven and prepare the baking dish as directed. Peel and core 4 apples, then cut each one into eighths. In a large frying pan, melt 2 tbsp unsalted butter over medium-high heat. Add the apples and cook, stirring, just until brown, about 5 minutes. Sprinkle with 2 tsp sugar and continue to cook, stirring often, just until caramelized, about 3 minutes longer. Spread evenly in the prepared baking dish. Prepare the pudding using cinnamon-raisin bread. Lay the slices over the apples, add the egg mixture, and bake for 35 minutes. Brush with warmed apple jelly and finish baking as directed.

BEVERAGES

MORNING COCKTAILS, JUICES,
SMOOTHIES & HOT DRINKS

When mixing up Bloody Marys for a crowd, set up a DIY bar and encourage guests to doctor their own drinks with a selection of seasonings and garnishes.

MORNING COCKTAILS

BLOODY MARY BAR

1 lemon, halved

4 cups (1 l) tomato juice

2 tsp Worcestershire sauce or A1 steak sauce

1–2 tsp horseradish

2 tsp celery salt

1 tsp cayenne pepper

½ tsp paprika

Freshly ground black pepper

2 cups (500 ml) vodka

Squeeze the juice from the lemon halves into a large pitcher. Add the tomato juice, Worcestershire sauce, horseradish, celery salt, cayenne, paprika, and a few grinds of black pepper and stir until thoroughly combined. Add the vodka and stir to combine.

Fill 6 rocks glasses or tumblers with ice and place on the bar. Encourage guests to pour their own drinks, add seasonings, and garnish as desired.

BAR SEASONING & GARNISH OPTIONS
hot sauce, salt and pepper, celery ribs with leaves, baby radishes, long pickle wedges, pickled asparagus spears, pickled green beans, fried bacon slices, cornichons, peperoncini, pickled onions, martini olives, and lime wedges, plus all of the above seasonings.

MAKES 6 SERVINGS

MICHELADA

1 tbsp plus 1 tsp coarse sea salt

2 tsp pure chili powder

6 limes

Ice cubes for serving

4 tsp Worcestershire sauce

Hot pepper sauce to taste

4 bottles (375 ml each) Mexican beer

Have ready 4 tall glasses or tumblers. Spread the salt and chili powder on a small, flat plate. Cut 2 of the limes into 4 wedges each. Run 1 lime wedge around the rim of each glass to moisten it, then dip the rim into the chile salt to coat it evenly. Reserve the remaining 4 lime wedges for garnish.

Juice the remaining 4 limes; you should have about ½ cup (125 ml) lime juice.

Fill each glass with several ice cubes. Add 2 tbsp of the lime juice, 1 tsp of the Worcestershire sauce, and a dash or two of hot pepper sauce to each glass. Pour 1 beer into each glass and stir gently. Garnish with a lime wedge and serve.

MAKES 4 SERVINGS

RAMOS FIZZ

¾ cup (180 ml) gin

¼ cup (60 ml) heavy cream

Juice of 4 lemons

4 large egg whites

8 drops orange flower water

¼ cup (50 g) superfine sugar

Ice cubes

Chill 4 tall glasses. In a blender, combine the gin, cream, lemon juice, egg whites, orange flower water, and superfine sugar and blend until smooth and frothy. Add enough ice to fill the blender three-fourths full. Remove the blender canister from the base, cover the canister tightly, and shake gently to cool the drink. Strain through a fine-mesh sieve into the chilled glasses and serve.

MAKES 4 SERVINGS

Note: This recipe calls for raw egg whites. While the incidence of bacteria in raw eggs is rare, anyone with a compromised immune system should use caution.

JUICES & SMOOTHIES

EACH MAKES ABOUT 2 SERVINGS

SUPER GREEN JUICE

2 Persian cucumbers + 1 green apple + 6 kale leaves + 2 cups (60 g) spinach + 3 ribs celery + 3 carrots

Cut the cucumbers and apple to fit the tube of a juicer. Place the cucumbers, apple, kale, spinach, celery, and carrots into the feeder of a juice extractor and run the machine. Pour into glasses and enjoy as soon as possible.

BEET-APPLE-COCONUT JUICE

4 red apples + 3 red beets + 1 cup (250 ml) coconut water

Cut the apples and beets to fit the tube of a juicer. Place the apples and beets into the feeder of a juice extractor and run the machine. Pour into glasses, stir in the coconut water, and enjoy as soon as possible.

CARROT SUNRISE JUICE

1 orange + ½ lemon + ¼ pineapple + 2 carrots

Peel the orange, lemon, and pineapple and cut to fit the tube of a juicer. Place the cut pieces and the carrots into the feeder of a juice extractor and run the machine. Pour into glasses and enjoy as soon as possible.

MANDARIN-GUAVA-STRAWBERRY JUICE

4 mandarin oranges + 1 lime + 6 guavas + 1 cup (150 g) strawberries

Peel the oranges, lime, and guavas and cut to fit the tube of a juicer. Place the oranges, lime, guavas, and strawberries into the feeder of a juice extractor and run the machine. Pour into glasses and enjoy as soon as possible.

HONEYDEW-KIWI COOLER

½ honeydew melon, seeds removed + 4 kiwifruits + 1 lime

Peel the melon, kiwifruits, and lime and cut to fit the tube of a juicer. Place the melon, kiwifruits, and lime into the feeder of a juice extractor and run the machine. Pour into glasses and enjoy as soon as possible.

GINGER-BERRY-POM JUICE

2 red apples + 2 tangerines, peeled + 2 cups (250 g) pomegranate seeds + 2 cups (250 g) raspberries + Knob of ginger, peeled

Cut the apples to fit the tube of a juicer. Place the apples, tangerines, pomegranate seeds, raspberries, and ginger into the feeder of a juice extractor and run the machine. Pour into glasses and enjoy as soon as possible.

TROPICAL SMOOTHIE

1 banana, quartered + 1½ cups (280 g) frozen mango cubes + ½ cup (90 g) frozen diced pineapple + ½ cup (125 g) low-fat vanilla yogurt + ½ cup (125 ml) fresh orange juice, or as needed

In a blender, combine the banana, mango, pineapple, yogurt, and orange juice, and blend until smooth, adding more orange juice if the mixture is too thick. Pour into glasses and serve.

BANANA-DATE PROTEIN SHAKE

2 ripe bananas, sliced and frozen + 4 pitted dates + ¼ cup (75 g) almond butter + ½ tsp ground cinnamon + ½ cup (125 ml) cold unsweetened almond milk + 1½ tbsp raw cacao powder

In a blender, combine the bananas, dates, almond butter, cinnamon, almond milk, and cacao powder and blend until smooth. Pour into glasses and serve.

HOT DRINKS

WHIPPED HOT CHOCOLATE

2 cups (500 ml) low-fat or whole milk
4 tsp unsweetened Dutch-process cocoa powder
4 tsp sugar
½ lb (250 g) bittersweet chocolate, finely chopped or grated
¼ tsp salt
¼ tsp ground cinnamon
Whipped cream for serving (optional)

In a small saucepan, combine the milk, cocoa powder, and sugar. Place over medium heat and heat, whisking until the sugar dissolves and the mixture is warmed through. Add the chocolate, salt, and cinnamon and whisk vigorously until the mixture is frothy, smooth, and very warm. Pour into coffee cups or mugs. Top with whipped cream, if using, and serve.

MAKES 4 SERVINGS

LEMON VERBENA & MINT TISANE

1 bunch fresh lemon verbena sprigs
1 bunch fresh mint
Sugar for serving (optional)

If desired, set aside 2 lemon verbena sprigs for garnish. In a teapot, combine the remaining lemon verbena sprigs and the mint. In a saucepan, bring 3 cups (750 ml) water to a boil over high heat. Pour into the teapot and let the tisane steep until it reaches the desired strength, 3–5 minutes.

Strain through a tea strainer or a fine-mesh sieve into 2 teacups. Garnish each cup with a lemon verbena sprig, if using, and serve. Pass the sugar at the table, if desired.

MAKES 2 SERVINGS

CHAI LATTE

1 cinnamon stick
4 green cardamom pods
4 black cardamom pods
10 whole cloves
2 peppercorns
5 thin slices peeled fresh ginger
⅔ cup (160 ml) whole milk
2 tbsp sugar
4 tsp Darjeeling tea leaves

In a saucepan, combine the cinnamon stick, cardamom pods, cloves, peppercorns, ginger, and 1½ cups (375 ml) water. Bring to a boil over medium heat. Cover, reduce the heat to low, and simmer until aromatic, about 10 minutes.

Add the milk and sugar and bring to a simmer over medium heat, stirring until the sugar dissolves. Stir in the tea leaves, remove from the heat, cover, and let stand until the chai reaches the desired strength, 3–5 minutes.

If you have a milk frother, pour half of the chai into a pitcher, froth it, then return it to the pan. Strain the chai through a fine-mesh sieve into 2 mugs, spooning foam onto the tops, and serve.

MAKES 2 SERVINGS

MATCHA LATTE

1–1½ tsp matcha powder
1 tbsp hot water
1–2 tsp honey or agave nectar, or to taste
¾ cup (180 ml) hot milk, frothed

Spoon the matcha powder into a cup. Add the hot water and whisk until no lumps remain, then whisk in the honey. Pour the frothed milk over the matcha into a teacup and serve.

MAKES 1 SERVING

BELLINI BAR

MAKES 6 SERVINGS

Put a few bottles of sparkling wine on ice, set out a selection of fruit purées and some pretty glasses, and your DIY bellini bar is complete. Each fruit blend makes about 1 cup (8 fl oz/250 ml) purée, or enough for a bottle's worth of sparkling wine.

Fruit purée of choice

1 bottle (750 ml) dry sparkling wine, Champagne, or Prosecco, chilled

Fresh fruit for garnish

Make one fruit purée at a time: In a blender, combine the fruit and sugar, and (if using) the brandy or lemon juice. Blend to a smooth purée. Taste and add more sugar if needed; the purée should be sweet but not overly sweet. Pour the purée into a small pitcher or carafe, straining it through a coarse sieve if a smooth consistency is desired.

Fill 6 Champagne flutes about one-third full with the fruit purée. Slowly fill the flutes with the sparkling wine. Stir briefly and serve, garnished with fresh fruit.

BLACKBERRY PURÉE
3 cups (375 g) blackberries
+ ⅓ cup (70 g) superfine sugar,
or to taste

PEAR PURÉE
4 pears, peeled, halved, cored,
and coarsely chopped + ¼ cup (50 g)
superfine sugar, or to taste
+ 1 tbsp pear brandy (optional)

STRAWBERRY PURÉE
2½ cups (400 g) halved strawberries
+ ¼ cup (50 g) superfine sugar, or to taste

PEACH PURÉE
4 ripe white or yellow peaches, peeled,
halved, pitted, and coarsely chopped
+ ¼ cup (50 g) superfine sugar
+ 1 tsp fresh lemon juice

BASIC RECIPES

HOLLANDAISE SAUCE

4 large egg yolks

2 tbsp fresh lemon juice

Salt and freshly ground pepper

1 cup (225 g) unsalted butter

To make the hollandaise sauce, in a blender, combine the egg yolks, lemon juice, ⅛ tsp salt, and a few grinds of pepper. In a small saucepan, melt the butter over medium heat. With the blender running, slowly add the warm melted butter and blend until the sauce is thick and smooth. Season to taste with salt and pepper. If the sauce is too thick, add a little water to thin it. Transfer the hollandaise sauce to a heatproof bowl. Cover and set over but not touching barely simmering water in a saucepan to keep warm until ready to use.

MAKES ABOUT 1½ CUPS (350 ML)

QUICK STRAWBERRY JAM

2 pints (600 g) strawberries, stemmed, cored, and sliced

1 cup (200 g) sugar

2 tbsp fresh lemon juice

Place a saucer in the freezer to chill.

In a saucepan, combine the strawberries, sugar, and lemon juice. Place over medium heat and bring to a boil, stirring constantly until the sugar dissolves. Reduce the heat to medium-low and cook, stirring occasionally, until the berries are tender and the juices thicken, about 10 minutes.

To test, remove the chilled saucer from the freezer. Spoon about 1 tsp of the strawberry liquid onto the saucer and let stand for 15 seconds. If the liquid thickens to a jamlike consistency, then the jam is ready. If not, cook for 1 to 2 minutes longer. Transfer to glass jars or other covered containers and let cool. The jam can be stored, covered, in the refrigerator for up to 10 days.

MAKES ABOUT 3 CUPS (700 ML)

LEMON CURD

1 large egg plus 4 large egg yolks

½ cup (100 g) sugar

⅓ cup (80 ml) fresh lemon juice

2 tbsp unsalted butter

In a heatproof bowl set over but not touching barely simmering water in a saucepan, whisk together the egg, egg yolks, sugar, and lemon juice. Cook, stirring constantly, until thickened, about 5 minutes. Remove from the heat, add the butter, and stir until incorporated. Strain through a fine-mesh sieve into another bowl. Cover with a piece of plastic wrap pressed directly on the surface of the curd and refrigerate until chilled. The curd can be stored in the refrigerator for up to 3 days or in the freezer for up to 1 month.

MAKES ABOUT 1 CUP (250 G)

STRAWBERRY-RHUBARB COMPOTE

4 cups (750 g) coarsely chopped rhubarb stalks

¼ cup (50 g) sugar

1½ cups (225 g) strawberries, stemmed, cored, and halved

In a saucepan, combine the rhubarb, sugar, and ¼ cup (60 ml) water. Place over medium heat and cook, stirring occasionally, until the mixture comes to a simmer and the rhubarb begins to release its liquid, about 10 minutes, then stir in the strawberries. Simmer gently, stirring occasionally, until the rhubarb is soft when pierced with a fork, about 10 minutes longer. Skim any foam off the top. Transfer to glass jars or other covered containers and let cool. The compote can be stored, covered, in the refrigerator for up to 10 days.

MAKES ABOUT 3 CUPS (700 ML)

BING CHERRY SYRUP

½ cup (100 g) firmly packed light brown sugar

½ cup (100 g) granulated sugar

1½ cups (280 g) pitted Bing cherries

1 tsp pure almond extract

In a saucepan, combine both sugars and 1 cup (250 ml) water. Place over high heat and bring to a boil, stirring constantly until the sugars dissolve. Boil for 5 minutes, stirring constantly. Add the cherries, reduce the heat to medium-low, and simmer until the cherries are tender, 8–10 minutes. Stir in the almond extract and simmer for 2 minutes longer. Let cool. Use right away, or cover and refrigerate for up to 4 days.

MAKES ABOUT 2 CUPS (480 ML)

BLUEBERRY SYRUP

6 cups (900 g) blueberries

1½ cups (300 g) sugar

1 tsp finely chopped lemon zest (optional)

3 tbsp fresh lemon juice

In a saucepan, combine the blueberries, sugar, lemon zest (if using), and ¾ cup (180 ml) water. Place over high heat and bring to a boil. Reduce the heat to medium-low and simmer, stirring occasionally, until the blueberries are plump and some have burst, about 10 minutes.

Set a fine-mesh sieve over a bowl. Transfer the blueberry mixture to the sieve and press on the solids with a wooden spoon to extract the liquid. Return the liquid to the saucepan, place over high heat, and bring to a boil. Reduce the heat to medium-low and simmer, stirring, until a light, syrupy consistency is reached, 2–5 minutes. Stir in the lemon juice. Let cool. Use right away, or cover and refrigerate for up to 4 days.

MAKES ABOUT 3 CUPS (700 ML)

VARIATIONS

Lavender-Blueberry Syrup Add 3 tbsp dried or ⅓ cup (20 g) fresh pesticide-free lavender flowers to the blueberries, sugar, and water.

Orange-Blueberry Syrup Substitute the same amount of finely chopped orange zest and fresh orange juice for the lemon zest and juice.

MAPLE-PEAR SAUCE

4 Anjou or Bartlett pears, cored and sliced

Grated zest of ½ lemon plus juice of 1 lemon

¼ cup (60 g) unsalted butter

1 cup (310 g) pure maple syrup

In a bowl, toss together the pears and lemon juice. In a saucepan, melt the butter over medium heat. Add the pears and cook, stirring occasionally, for 2 minutes. Add the lemon zest, maple syrup, and ¼ cup (60 ml) water and simmer until the pears are tender, about 6 minutes. Using a slotted spoon, transfer the pears to a bowl and keep warm. Raise the heat to high and boil until the liquid is reduced to a syrup, about 10 minutes. Return the pears to the syrup. Use right away, or cover and refrigerate for up to 1 day.

MAKES ABOUT 2 CUPS (480 ML)

CREAM CHEESE ICING

1½ cups (180 g) confectioners' sugar

2 oz (60 g) cream cheese, at room temperature

2 tbsp unsalted butter, at room temperature

½ tsp pure vanilla extract

Grated zest of 1 orange

About ¼ cup (60 ml) whole milk

Sift the confectioners' sugar into the clean bowl of a stand mixer and add the cream cheese, butter, vanilla, and orange zest. Beat on low speed (preferably using the paddle attachment) until crumbly. Gradually beat in enough of the milk to make a thick but pourable icing.

MAKES ABOUT 1 CUP (225 G)

HONEY BUTTER

¼ cup (60 g) unsalted butter, at room temperature

2 tbsp good-quality honey

Salt

In a bowl, combine the butter and honey and season with salt. Using an electric mixer, beat on medium speed until creamy and fluffy, about 2 minutes. Wrap in plastic wrap and refrigerate until ready to use.

MAKES ABOUT ⅓ CUP (90 G)

CIDER-MAPLE BUTTER

¼ cup (60 ml) apple cider

¼ cup (60 g) unsalted butter, at room temperature

2 tbsp pure maple syrup

Salt

In a small saucepan, bring the apple cider to a boil over medium-high heat. Cook until the cider is reduced to 1 tbsp, about 2 minutes. Let cool to room temperature.

In a bowl, combine the reduced apple cider, butter, and maple syrup and season with salt. Using an electric mixer, beat on medium speed until creamy and fluffy, about 2 minutes. Wrap in plastic wrap and refrigerate until ready to use.

MAKES ABOUT ⅓ CUP (90 G)

SUGAR-AND-SPICE BUTTER

¼ cup (60 g) unsalted butter, at room temperature

2 tbsp confectioners' sugar

¾ tsp ground cinnamon

¼ tsp ground ginger

Salt

In a bowl, combine the butter, confectioners' sugar, cinnamon, and ginger and season with salt. Using an electric mixer, beat on medium speed until creamy and fluffy, about 2 minutes. Wrap in plastic wrap and refrigerate until ready to use.

MAKES ABOUT ⅓ CUP (90 G)

MAPLE-CRANBERRY BUTTER

¼ cup (30 g) fresh or thawed frozen cranberries

2 tbsp pure maple syrup

½ cup (120 g) unsalted butter, at room temperature

In a saucepan, combine the cranberries and maple syrup. Place over low heat and cook, stirring, until the cranberries have softened and popped, about 5 minutes. Let cool completely. Transfer to a bowl, add the butter, and beat with a wooden spoon to combine. Spoon the flavored butter onto a sheet of waxed paper and shape it into a log. Wrap in plastic wrap and refrigerate until ready to use.

MAKES ABOUT ⅔ CUP (150 G)

BASIC DOUGHNUT GLAZE

2 cups (250 g) confectioners' sugar

¼ cup (60 ml) whole milk, plus more if needed

1½ tsp pure vanilla extract or other extract such as lavender, raspberry, or coconut

¼ tsp salt

2–3 drops food coloring (optional)

In a bowl, stir together the confectioners' sugar, milk, vanilla, and salt until smooth and well blended. Add more milk, 1 tsp at a time, if needed for a thinner consistency. If a tinted glaze is desired, stir in food coloring until blended. Use right away.

MAKES ABOUT ¾ CUP (180 ML)

CHOCOLATE DOUGHNUT GLAZE

¼ cup (60 ml) hot water

¼ lb (125 g) semisweet chocolate

2 cups (250 g) confectioners' sugar

5 tbsp (75 g) unsalted butter

1½ tsp pure vanilla extract

¼ tsp salt

In a heatproof bowl set over but not touching barely simmering water in a saucepan, combine the hot water, chocolate, confectioners' sugar, butter, vanilla, and salt. Cook, stirring occasionally, until the chocolate and butter are melted, 2–3 minutes. Remove from the heat and stir until smooth and well blended. Use right away.

MAKES ABOUT 1⅓ CUPS (320 ML)

STRAWBERRY DOUGHNUT GLAZE

2 cups (250 g) confectioners' sugar

½ cup (155 g) strawberry syrup, or ½ cup (155 g) strawberry jelly thinned with 2 tbsp water

Pinch of salt

In a bowl, stir together the confectioners' sugar, strawberry syrup, and salt until smooth and well blended. Use right away.

MAKES ABOUT 1 CUP (240 ML)

LEMON DOUGHNUT GLAZE

½ cup (125 g) plain whole-milk Greek or regular yogurt

Grated zest of 1 lemon

¼ tsp salt

1 cup (125 g) confectioners' sugar

In a bowl, stir together the yogurt, lemon zest, and salt. Add the confectioners' sugar and stir until smooth and well blended.

MAKES ABOUT ⅔ CUP (160 ML)

MAPLE DOUGHNUT GLAZE

1¾ cups (200 g) confectioners' sugar

3 tbsp whole milk

2 tsp pure maple extract

In a bowl, stir together the confectioners' sugar, milk, and maple extract until smooth and well blended. Use right away.

MAKES ABOUT ½ CUP (120 ML)

CORNMEAL TART DOUGH

2 cups (250 g) all-purpose flour, plus more for dusting

½ cup (75 g) cornmeal

½ tsp baking powder

¼ tsp salt

¾ cup (180 g) cold unsalted butter, cut into pieces

2 large egg yolks

3–4 tbsp ice water

In a food processor, combine the flour, cornmeal, baking powder, and salt and pulse briefly to mix. Add the butter and pulse until the mixture resembles coarse crumbs. In a small bowl, whisk together the egg yolks and 3 tbsp of the ice water. Gradually add the egg mixture, pulsing just until the dough comes together, adding 1 tbsp more water if needed. (Alternatively, to mix the dough by hand, stir together the flour mixture in a large bowl, use a pastry blender to cut in the butter, and then stir in the egg mixture until blended.)

Dump the dough out onto a lightly floured surface and knead gently into a mound. Wrap in plastic wrap, flatten into a disk, and refrigerate for at least 30 minutes or up to 3 days.

On a lightly floured surface, roll out the dough into a rectangle about 11 by 14 inches (28 by 35 cm), lifting the dough and dusting the surface with flour as needed. Fold the dough in half and transfer to an 8-by-11-inch (20-by-28-cm) rectangular tart pan. Unfold the dough over the pan, fitting it into the bottom and sides of the pan and patching the dough as needed. Using kitchen scissors, trim the dough, leaving a 1-inch (2.5-cm) overhang. Fold the overhanging dough in against the pan sides, pressing it to form a rim. Refrigerate for at least 30 minutes, or cover with plastic wrap and refrigerate for up to 3 days. Bake as directed in your recipe or in a 375°F (190°C) oven for about 30 minutes total.

MAKES ENOUGH DOUGH TO FIT ONE 8-BY-11-INCH (20-BY-28-CM) RECTANGULAR TART PAN OR ONE 9-INCH (23-CM) ROUND TART PAN

SINGLE-CRUST FLAKY PIE DOUGH

1¼ cups (160 g) all-purpose flour

¼ tsp salt

½ tsp sugar (optional; omit if making a savory dish)

7 tbsp (105 g) very cold unsalted butter, cut into cubes

5 tbsp (80 ml) ice water, plus more as needed

In a food processor, combine the flour, salt, and sugar (if using) and pulse 2 or 3 times to mix evenly. Sprinkle the butter over the top and pulse for a few seconds, or just until the butter is slightly broken up into the flour but still in visible pieces. Evenly sprinkle the water over the flour mixture, then process just until the mixture starts to come together. Stop the machine and squeeze a piece of dough. If it crumbles, add more of the water, 1 tbsp at a time, and pulse just until the dough holds together when pinched.

Dump the dough into a large lock-top plastic bag and press into a flat disk. Refrigerate the dough for at least 30 minutes or up to 1 day, or freeze for up to 1 month.

MAKES ENOUGH FOR ONE 9-INCH (23-CM) SINGLE-CRUST PIE OR TART

INDEX

THE BREAKFAST BIBLE

Conceived and produced by Weldon Owen, Inc.
In collaboration with Williams Sonoma, Inc.
3250 Van Ness Avenue, San Francisco, CA 94109

A WELDON OWEN PRODUCTION
1150 Brickyard Cove Road
Richmond, CA 94801
www.weldonowen.com

Copyright © 2017 Weldon Owen International.
and Williams Sonoma, Inc.
All rights reserved, including the right of
reproduction in whole or in part in any form.

Printed in China

First printed in 2017
10 9

Library of Congress Cataloging-in-Publication
data is available.

ISBN: 978-1-68188-291-8

WELDON OWEN INTERNATIONAL
President & Publisher Roger Shaw
SVP, Sales & Marketing Amy Kaneko

Associate Publisher Amy Marr
Senior Editor Lisa Atwood

Creative Director Kelly Booth
Art Director Marisa Kwek
Designer Alexandra Zeigler
Senior Production Designer Rachel Lopez Metzger
Production Designer Howie Severson

Associate Production Director Michelle Duggan
Imaging Manager Don Hill

Photographer Sang An
Food Stylist Lillian Kang
Prop Stylist Angela Romero

ACKNOWLEDGMENTS

Weldon Owen wishes to thank the following people for their generous support
in producing this book: Kris Balloun, Justin Barrett, Jane Bonacci, Peggy Fallon,
Ian Green, Amy Hatwig, Veronica Laramie, Rachel Markowitz, Alexis Mersel,
Carolyn Miller, Elizabeth Parson, Colleen Proppé, Sharon Silva, and Tamara White.